DEVELOPMENTAL ECONOMICS

From Gender to Natural Resources

DEVELOPMENTAL ECONOMICS
From Gender to Natural Resources

Dr. Parikshit Sahu

Delta Book World
New Delhi-110 002

ISBN: 978-93-85719-18-9
First Published in 2021

Published by **Abhishek Goel** on behalf of

Delta Book World
G-4, Prahlad House
4832/24, Ansari Road
New Delhi - 110 002 (India)

Tel.: 011-4707 2321
E-mail: deltabookworld@gmail.com
Website: www.kaveribooks.com

PRINTED IN INDIA

Dedicated To

My Heavenly Parents

Late Shri Ananda Charan Sahu

&

Late Smt. Malati Devi

Foreword

Lately, the world has been experiencing unprecedented uncertainty – be it in the form of political turmoil or tension due to socio-economic and environmental upheavals. An immediate consequence that is manifest in every stratum of social and economic developments is the extent of instability and the sub-optimal responses of our system due to heterogenous degree of misinformed policy decisions. Dr. Parikshit Sahu's book is a reflection of these mounting challenges that prompt us to delve deep into various social, educational and development problems in order for us to develop our own strategic solutions. Indeed, the most difficult problems that surround us, often find solutions in simple strategies. Dr. Sahu has attempted to bring us closer to that simplicity.

Dr. Parikshit Sahu is bringing a reflective book entitled 'Developmental Economics: From Gender to Natural Resources' in the above context and I am very happy to see that the book has a number of chapters that discuss the above problems in depth. At the same time, he provides ways to resolve the nagging problems and create a sustainable world that can co-move with the unconquerable uncertainties in multidimensions and our own localised strategies of self-reliance and value the basics. I am sure, the readers will gain immensely from reading the various carefully drafted chapters which provide both analytical logics and robust empirical support.

I wish the author as well as the readers the very best.

Professor Tapas Mishra
PhD Economics (UCL, Belgium),
M.Phil (Economics) (Delhi School of Economics)
Professor and Head of Banking and Finance
Southampton Business School,
University of Southampton, UK
Associate Editor:
Cliometrica; European Journal of Finance

Acknowledgements

For publication of this book, I would like to give thanks to my teachers Prof. Kumar B. Das, Prof. Padmaja Mishra and late. Prof. Adwaita Mohanty of Utkal University and present senior Professor, Dr. Himanshu Kumar Rout of A & A Economics, Utkal University. No words can adequately express my gratitude to Sri Manas Ranjan Debata, Additional Secretary to Government, PR & DW Department, Government of Odisha for generating a perennial interest in me for this publication. I must give thanks to Prof. Tapas Mishra, Professor and Head of Finance and Econometrics, Southampton Business School Southampton University, UK for his inspiration for this publication. Moreover, I never forget the support of my dearest friend Mr. Akhil Kumar Mishra, IIS, Director, Regional Outreach Bureau (Erstwhile DFP), Bhubaneswar, Ministry of I&B, Govt. of India for this new creation. Similarly, I would like to give my sincere thanks to Dr. Mahesh Ranjan Debata, Assistant Professor, School of International Studies, Jawaharlal Nehru University for his moral support for this publication.

It would be a pride to appreciate the contribution of my wife Smt. Sasmita Sahoo, who inspired confidence in me to prosper in future against all trials and tribulations. Moreover, it would be injustice, if I will not give my sincere thanks to my beloved son MMP Shubhrakant, who always takes pride in my achievements in all aspects of life and imbibes extra-terrestrial effect on me.

Further, definitely, I would like to extend my heartiest thanks to Principal Secretary, PR & DW Department, Govt. of Odisha, Director, Joint Director, Assistant Directors and all my colleagues of SIRD & PR for their support in this regard. I would like to acknowledge my hearty thanks to Mr. Abhishek Goel, the publisher of this book for his splendid works to bring this book for the readers in right time. Last but not the least; I would like to extend my debt to those friends and relatives who have rendered their altruistic support directly or indirectly for this new creation.

I shall welcome any suggestions from all quarters that may improve the utility and usefulness of this book. I will feel amply rewarded if this piece of book motivates a band of young development professionals, researchers, economists, government officials and the like on their way to work for the betterment and development of the people in particular and the nation or economy in general.

Bhubaneswar

Hanuman Jayanti
Dated: 13th April 2020

Dr. Parikshit Sahu

Preface

The economic development and economic growth are the frequently used buzzwords by the development professionals, economists, researchers and sociologists. Economic growth is the increase in goods and services produced by an economy or nation in a specific period of time. The increase in the country's production of goods and services is steady and stable and may be reasoned by an improvement in the quality of education, improvements in technology or in a value addition in goods and services by every sector of the economy. Economic development can create wealthier and healthier opportunities in the sectors of education, healthcare, employment, the conservation of the environment and moreover the improvement in the standard of living of the people. The standard of living includes various things like safe drinking water; improve sanitation systems, healthcare facilities, the universalisation of elementary education to improve literacy rate, eradication of poverty, balanced transport networks, increase in employment opportunities, improvement in need based infrastructural facilities etc. Therefore, an increase in economic development is more necessary for an economy to achieve the status of a developed nation. Economic Development is considered as a multidimensional phenomenon and by synchronized development it can be understood that all the sectors must grows simultaneously with an objective to touch the upper steps of the ladder of developed nation.

The book "Developmental Economics: From Gender to Natural Resources" has nine chapters. Here, in this book all the chapters have been dedicated to focus on the theme of Globalization, Natural Resources Management (NRM), Women Development, Forest Rights Act (FRA), Community Based Forest Management, Human Resource Development (HRD), Social sectors development like education, health care and so on. It can be stated that individually all these chapters are like the indifference curves in economics of different sectors of Indian economy with some comparative taste with global scenario as well as the state economies. These analysis placed in the book tries to analyze the problems, issues, concerns, policy implications as well as the policy recommendations to the effect consistently and comprehensively in consonance with their relative importance in view of the degree of necessities of the development issues of the governments (Union and States).

The economic and social sectors development aligned with poverty alleviation are the main themes and the central concerns of the government. These concerns of the economy prompts to different complementary strategies like fulfilling the basic needs of the people, reducing economic imbalances, enhancing income, increasing employment, maintaining quality education, management of natural as well as human resources, development of the status of women and other marginalized communities and the like. These essences have been incorporated in the book perfectly through different chapters.

Contents

Abbreviations

AIBP	- Accelerated Irrigation Benefit Programme
CADP	- Command Area Development Programme
CAGR	- Compound Annual Growth Rate
CBNRM	- Community Based Natural Resource Management
CCIs	- Child Care Institutions,
CFM	- Community Forest Management
CFR	- Community Forest Resources/Community Forest Right
CFR P & MC	- Community Forest Right Protection & Management Committee
CNCP	- Children in Need of Care and Protection
CSD	- Campaign for Survival and Dignity
DDP	- Desert Development Programme
DLC	- District Level Committee
DoLR	- Department of Land Resources
DPAP	- Drought Prone Areas Programme
DRDA	- District Rural Development Agency
DSSOs	- District Social Security Officers
EAS	- Employment Assurance Scheme
FDI	- Foreign Direct Investment
FGD	- Focused Group Discussion

FPC	- Forest Protection Committee
FRA	- Forest Right Act
FRC	- Forest Right Committee
FWP	- Food for Work Programme
GES	- Global Entrepreneurship Summit
GGY	- Gopabandhu Gramin Yojana
GIS	- Geographic Information System
GMP	- Good Manufacturing Practices
GNP	- Gross Domestic Products
GPS	- Global Positioning System
GSDP	- Gross State Domestic Product
GSVA	- Gross State Value Added
GVA	- Gross Value Added
IADP	- Intensive Agricultural District Programme
IAP	- Integrated Action Plan
IAY	- Indira Awaas Yojana
ICCPR	- International Covenant on Civil and Political Rights
ICPS	- Integrated Child Protection Scheme,
IEC	- Information-Education and Communication
IFR	- Individual Forest Right
IPC	- Indian Penal Code
IRDP	- Integrated Rural Development Programme
IWDP	- Integrated Wasteland Development Programme
IWMP	- Integrated Watershed Management Programme
JFM	- Joint Forest Management
JFMC	- Joint Forest Management Committee
JFPC	- Joint Forest Protection Committee
JKPBA	- Jammu & Kashmir Prevention of Beggary
JRY	- Jawahar Rozgar Yojana

MFDA	- Marginal Farmers Development Agency
MFP	- Minor Forest Product
MGNREGA	- Mahatma Gandhi National Rural Employment Guarantee Act
MGNREGS	- Mahatma Gandhi National Rural Employment Guarantee Scheme
MMA	- Macro Management of Agriculture
MNP	- Minimum Needs Programme
MoTA	- Ministry of Tribal Affairs
NGOs	- Non-Governmental Organizations
NIRD	- National Institute of Rural Development
NREGS	- National Rural Employment Guarantee Scheme
NREP	- National Rural Employment Programme
NRHM	- National Rural Health Mission,
NTFP	- Non-Timber Forest Produce
NWDPRA	- National Watershed Development Programme for Rainfed Areas
OPLE	- Odisha Prevention of Land Encroachment Act
OTFD	- Other Traditional Forest Dwellers
PBA	- Bombay Prevention of Begging Act
PMAY(G)	- Pradhan Mantri Awas Yojna (Gramin)
PMGSY	- Pradhan Mantri Gram Sadak Yojana
PRA	- Participatory Rural Appraisal
PRIs	- Panchayati Raj Institutions
PURA	- Provision of Urban Amenities to Rural Areas
RIDF	- Rural Infrastructure Development Fund
RLEGP	- Rural Landless Employment Guarantee Programme
RL	- Revenue Land
RLTAP	- Revised Long Term Action Plan
ROR	- Record of Right

RSVY	- Rastriya Sam Vikas Yojna
RTE	- Right to Education
RVP	- River Valley Projects
SDGs	- Sustainable Development Goals
SDLC	- Sub Divisional Level Committee
SFDA	- Small Farmers Development Agency
SGSY	- Swarnajayanti Gram Swarozgar Yojana
SHGs	- Self Help Groups
SLMC	- State Level Monitoring Committee
SPMRM	- Shyama Prasad Mukherji Rurban Mission
SSEPD	- Social Security and Empowerment of Persons with Disabilities
TNCs	- Transnational Corporations
UEE	- Universalisation of Elementary Education
VDC	- Village Development Committee
VSS	- Vana Samrakshana Samiti
WDPSCA	- Watershed Development Programme for Shifting Cultivation Areas
WODC	- Western Odisha Development Council

1

Quality Primary Education for Girls and Socio-Economic Development in India

INTRODUCTION

"Education is a fundamental human right and essential for the exercise of all other human rights. It promotes individual freedom and empowerment and yields important development benefits. Yet millions of children and adults remain deprived of educational opportunities, many as a result of poverty".[1] Out of different branches of social sector, primary education, as the principal component it has to play the pivotal role in achieving the Universalisation of Elementary Education (UEE) and sound economic growth of the society. Education is a vibrant mechanism in developing human ability that provides the instruments for emancipation from ignorance and subjugation. It is both the origin and outcomes of development. Imparting quality education of education is now an issue of global concern.

Mobilizing resources towards girl's education has the potential to produce the highest returns for economic development and that gender disparities in education have an adverse impact not just on girls, but on their entire families and societies. In light of the above, at the World Education Forum, Dakar 2000[2] nations around the world agreed on two goals relating to prioritizing girls education. The first goal is to ensure that all children; particularly girls have access to and complete free and compulsory education of good quality by 2015 and the second goal is to eliminate gender disparity in primary and secondary education by 2005 and achieving gender equality in education by 2015, with a focus on ensuring girls full and equal access to, achievement, in basic education.

The main indicator of the quality of elementary education can be analyzed in terms of its products – the learners' outcomes both in scholastic and co-scholastic areas. The factors correlated with the success are aligned with the conditions of learning and learning environment that are occasionally considered as indicators of quality of primary education.

UNDERSTANDING QUALITY IN EDUCATION

A reliable measure of quality of education is whether pupils are learning effectively, improving their knowledge, skills and abilities; widening their experience and growing socially and morally or not.

Since the inception of the educational system we are discussing the concept of quality education, but there is no mutual consent among the educational researchers regarding the meaning of the quality in education but there are many methods to measure it.

In the perspective of school effectiveness, the notion of quality is coupled with the effectiveness of teaching-learning processes. Some educationists are of the opinion to shift the concept from "Education For All" to "Quality Education For All". To them no-detention policy at primary level in several countries does not extirpate the dropout rate. Moreover, they stressed on the budge of academic learning to value based learning as an emerging dimension of education. It has well proved that "failure of education in the 20th century was not failure to teach science but failure to teach human values".

OCTAGON OF QUALITY EDUCATION

A school that enables all children to attend regularly, learn effectively and graduate successfully that must require at least eight components which is technically called as octagon of quality education.

These are as follows:

1. Competent and Motivated teachers,
2. Active learning methods, accompanied by appropriate learning/teaching aids,
3. Active participation of children and parents in school governance,
4. Safe, sound and effective learning environment,
5. Relevant curriculum i.e appropriate and relevant to local needs.
6. Student's preparedness- Health status, high learning time, parents' support, reasonable level of holistic development.
7. Empowered and supportive school leadership and
8. Acceptable level of Government budget allocation/strong supervisory support.

RIGHT TO EDUCATION (RTE) AND PROVISIONS FOR GIRLS

At different levels, there are some barriers on the path of girl education which have some significant impact for their educational and social development. They are as follows;

At household/community level there are some barriers for the girl children to be educated. In this context, it is the moral responsibility of every parent/guardian to inculcate the value of girl's education and the effect of sending their children to school.

Both physical and social factors are affecting girls' children to participate in schooling process. Therefore, the barrier free access is necessary to ensure this.

At system level, RTE mandates the appropriate government and local authorities to provide for children access to elementary schools within the denied area or limits of neighborhood. At policy level also every child aged 6 to 14 shall have a right to provision of free Compulsory, equitable quality education. It has been observed that the enrolment of girls in primary education system have been increased due to the government interventions and incentives through different flagship programmes on education.

WOMEN'S EDUCATION IN INDIA

Previously about 300 BC, there was virtually no education for women in India. Only women from higher strata were given some education at home. However, there was serious social resistance. Education to women was considered as a disgrace. The idea and benefits in providing education to girl children never entered into the minds of parents. According to the report of the National Committee on Women's Education (1959)[3], It cannot be denied that the general picture of the education of women was the most unsatisfactory and women received practically no formal instruction whatever, except for the little domestic instruction that was available to the daughter of the upper class families.

Previously, it was believed that women should aspire to become good wives and mothers, not intellectuals, doctors, lawyers etc. Women used to perform merely the domestic activities. They had been prohibited to speak in public. The main hindrance in the women education in India is rural residence, low caste, low economic standing combined with the traditional attitude towards women education as a whole. Due to these obstacles, educating the girls became unreachable.

SCENARIO OF GIRLS EDUCATION IN INDIA

India is a democratic country. The main canons of

democracy are equality, liberty fraternity and justice. In a democratic system, all men are born equal and are entitled to enjoy equal rights without any discrimination. In this backdrop, the wellbeing of girls needs special attention. Any inequity between the education of boys and girls should not be tolerable.

The tribulations of non-association and non-retention of girls at all levels of education is clearly visible and its proportion is higher at the primary level.

Girl's education in India has been experiencing multiple area specific issues that need special attention. The principal problem is the problem of wastage and stagnation. There are numerous grounds accountable for wastage in education at primary level; particularly in case of girls.

Attempts have been made to provide primary education to all children in India within the age brackets of 6 to 14 years with reference to girl's education. Governments at all levels have been trying a lot to reach at the goal of UEE. The problem is so acute that in spite of our several attempts we atr not yet been able to achieve that goal. The causes of the problems for the same may be educational, social and economic. The educational causes may be analyzed under the heads of poor infrastructure facilities, poor quality of teaching, defective nature of curricula and language difficulties etc. Similarly, social problems are illiteracy of parents, disinterest in education of girls, caste feeling and communal differences and lack of school community relationship.

TREND OF DEVELOPMENT OF PRIMARY EDUCATION FOR WOMEN IN ODISHA

- Since long back, there was no system of any kind for the education of women except domestic education. In the absence of government endeavour, the missionaries had made attempts after 1822, to recognize the requirement of education for women against all adverse factors.

- By 1882, the number of girls studying in mixed schools was 1623. However, the then government encouraged for the expansion of girls' education in mixed schools. Even, girl students were not being allowed to be awarded scholarships for their proficiency in mixed schools.
- Nevertheless, the condition of girls' education in South Odisha was not satisfactory. A beginning was made in 1875 with two Municipal girls' school one for the Muslim and another for the Hindus at Berhampur of Ganjam district. A few private bodies in South Odisha were taking interest in girls' education.
- In Odisha, the change came in after Hunter Commission Report, 1882 in which the encouragement for the expansion of girls' education came from Local and Municipal Board from different districts.
- In an Educational Conference held at Shimla In 1901, it was decided to set up more government schools for women, which were to be the model schools for other private agencies.
- To fulfill the necessity of the trained women teachers' three training schools were opened one at Cuttack and other two in Balasore, which were started by the Christian Missionaries during the year 1902-07.
- By the year 1905, the total number of girls' primary schools was 259 with an enrolment of 6894 girls, but 9009 girls were studying in boy's primary schools. Really, most of the parents were very traditional and apathetic to caters the same care and interest to educate their female children than that of boys.
- The Educational Policy of Government of India in 1904 gave an incentive for the expansion of girls' education. By 1905, there were four aided M. E. Schools only for girls under the management of American Baptist Mission after the separation of Bihar and Odisha from Bengal. In

1912, no such eye-catching improvement was visible in girl's education.

- According to the Government of India Resolution-1913, educational policy gave top priority to the educational qualification of the teachers. Accordingly, steps were taken in Bihar and Odisha for raising the general qualification and stipend of the female teachers.
- The then curriculum was not well suited to girls and certain new subjects were introduced from the standpoint of the girls. Subsequently, some educational administration structure had changed.
- In 1929, Hartong Committee recommended for the gradual introduction of compulsion for girl's education, appointment of lady teachers and inspectresses.
- In March 1930, Governor of Bihar and Odisha issued a resolution laying stress on the extended educational facilities for co-education for the increase of literacy among girls. Therefore, the government followed the policy of avoiding the opening of separate girl's primary schools as far as practicable.
- In South Odisha, the girls' education was in rearward as compared to boys education.
- After the separation of Odisha as a province in 1936, regarding the importance and utility of girl's education was an outstanding feature. The number of primary schools for girls' reduced from 421 in 1936-37 to 206 by 1946-47. Accordingly, the enrolment also decreased. However, in the mixed-schools the enrolment status was increased from 39993 in 1936 to 55647 by 1946-47.
- After independence, the need of girl's education and the whole outlook of the people were completely changed. To accelerate the progress of girls' education different measures were taken keeping in view the needs of independent India and its constitutional provisions for the expansion of girl's education.

- In the year 1947-48, there were only 192 girls primary schools with an enrolment of 9076 and was increased to 219 with 10871 pupils by the year 1950-51. During that period, girl's number in the co-educational institutions increased from 63474 to 91273.
- The problems and issues of women education were examined by the Central Committees; such as National Committee on Women's Education, 1958-59 appointed under the Chairmanship of Durgabhai Desmukh, National Council of Women Education, 1962, appointed under the Chairmanship of Hansa Mehta and Bhakta Vatsalm Committee in 1962.
- As the aim of universalisation of education in the state was solely to bring more girls to schools a number of measures, such as supply of free textbooks and Teaching Learning Materials (TLMs), free supply of school uniform to girls, residential quarters for women teachers etc. were taken by government. Besides that Sevasharam and Ashram schools were established for the girls from backward community.
- The NPE-1986, gave the message that education is an agent that could bring about basic changes in the position of women. Therefore, the state government adopted multi disciplinary approach and made interventions to raise the economic and social status of women and prepare them to stand at par with men. In order to accelerate the progress of girl's education the state government have introduced DPEP in the tribal districts where literacy of women is very low.

AREA SPECIFIC ISSUES; DISTURBING GIRLS EDUCATION IN ODISHA

Some area specific issues that disturbing girl's education in Odisha are like ill health of the child, teasing by classmates, rigorous corporal punishment, lack of individual attention on the part of the teacher, child labor, poor adolescent health, early marriage, immigration, child trafficking, child abuse, refugee, socio-cultural taboo, poor adolescent health, practice of Ghicha marriage (marriage by force) in Munda, Majhi and Gond community, siblings care, family migration (brick bhati), sexual harassment, apathetic attitude towards girls, muslim minority community, Naxalite affected, safety and security of girls, highly prone to disaster like flood, cyclone, lightening etc., trafficking, child labour, beggary, lack of awareness, seasonal absenteeism for mahula collection, girls engaged in household work, female foeticide and the like.

MEASURES TO PROMOTE WOMEN'S EDUCATION IN INDIA

National Committee on Women's Education suggested some points for the improvement of girls' education:

(i) Providing school facilities, opening of new schools, bringing schools within the reach of children, starting girls' section in boys' schools and condensed course for adult women etc.;

(ii) Improving the existing schools infrastructure and schooling process;

(iii) Making education free;

(iv) Educating public opinion;

(v) Providing other convenience and inducement like adjustment of school timings and vacation to suit local needs and conditions, free mid-day meals, free medical and health facilities for the school children, establishment of crèches etc.;

(vi) Introducing female inspecting officer;

(vii) Introduction of shift system for boys and girls in the same school building, where co-education is not acceptable;

(viii) Appointment of school mothers in mixed schools;

(ix) Establishment of nursery and pre-primary schools;

EDUCATION AND SOCIAL CHANGE

Education can act as an epitome of social change and social development. Moreover, education can initiate the social transformation by changing the outlook and attitude of man.

The traditional educational institutions and teachers used to show a specific way of life to the students and education was more a means of social control than an instrument of social change. The educational institutions in modern era do not stress upon the transformation of the way of life to the students. However, present education system aims at imparting knowledge. Education can brought about extraordinary changes in every aspect of men's life. This process that enables every individual to participate effectively in all the activities of society will contribute positively for the progress of society.

EDUCATION AND ECONOMIC GROWTH AND DEVELOPMENT

Education is indispensable to economic development. An appropriate educational system can endorse not only economic development but prompts to enhance productivity, and increase per capital income and the national income of the country as well.

The affiliation of education with economic growth has been the crux of economic analysis. Both Adam Smith in the 18th century and Alfred Marshall in the 19th century have given the tricks that how individual investments in "education" influence the wealth of nations. The adjacent cycle can justify the fact properly. Prior to the nineteenth century, systematic investment in human capital was not considered as much important in any country. During the 20th century, education, skills, and the technique of acquisition of knowledge have become fundamental factors of individual as well as nation's productivity. When the effective investment will be made in educating girls and women in developing country, it will create a multiplier effect for the family including better family health and nutrition, improved birth spacing, lower infant and child mortality, and enhanced educational attainment of children. The research explained that not a single country has achieved a sustainable economic development without considerable investment in human capital. Asymmetrical education system has a negative impact on per capita income in most countries. It is a fact that the investment in human capital will be fruitless, if people cannot use education in competition and open markets. The larger competitive in markets will follow the greater prospects for using education and skills.

RECOMMENDATIONS AND IMPLICATIONS

- It has seen that most of the children leave the school at any stage before their graduation. So the country as a whole and the states in particular should own sincere belongingness to solve the problems of non-involvement and non- retention of the girl students at primary level to create an educated society.
- Though girls and women have made much educational gains in recent years, there was a great gap between the education of men and women, but still have a long way to go before their historic educational disadvantage is eradicated.
- Some interrelated policies may be adopted in this line i.e promoting more competition, so that parental demand will create strong incentives to individual schools; autonomy in local decision making, so that individual schools and their leaders will take actions to promote student achievement; and, an accountability system that identifies good school performance and leads to rewards based on this.
- Teacher's salaries and types of engagement(like contractual), teacher rationalization, area specific micro

planning, introduction of mother-tongue based multi-lingual education and so on should be taken care of to improve the quality in primary education. The reasons of never-been-enrolled and drop-out should also be thoroughly analyzed so as to develop strategies to bring them back to school.

- For student's retention the school environment should be child friendly and hazard free. School infrastructure should be also conducive for girl students.
- Involvement of parents and community is an important aspect of civil society involvement.
- The governments at both ends i.e union and state should give priority to the education for girls.
- In Government of India, a department for women's education should be created in the Ministry of Human Resource Development for proper management of girl's education, a Director of Women's Education may be engaged in each state.
- In rural as well as tribal areas, education of girls' may be given more encouragement through different types of incentives to girls.
- Girl students should be provided training facilities on a liberal and priority basis.
- More seats in various services (central as well as state level) should be reserved for them.
- Educational outcomes need to be identified and quantified at the beginning of each academic year and need to be shared with the community to assess their expectation from the school.
- The school annual academic plan should clearly focus on achievable quality parameters. Quantified targets are possible only with scientific assessment and evaluation of each student.

- The curriculum and syllabus should be framed in area specific and need based manner to cater the local need of the pupils.
- Regular internal assessments and periodic external assessments should be conducted and these results should be communicated to the community for further course of action.
- Involvement of parents and community needs to be benchmarked to ensure greater accountability and educational outcomes.

CONCLUSION

The progress of women's education is a matter of concern after independence. Girls cannot be deprived of education at any cost and greater attention should be paid on problems of training and development of women. Now-a-days the girl's from inaccessible areas and weaker section of society are being encouraged to receive education. Government of India realized that education of girls is the most powerful tool of change of position in society. Education will reduce inequalities and will act as a means to improve their status within the family. To encourage the education of women at all levels and to bring more girls, especially from marginalized families for mainstreaming in education, the government at all level is providing innumerable assistances through different plans and programmes to accomplish the main objectives of Education for All (EFA) in India.

NOTES

1. United Nations Educational Scientific and Cultural Organization (UNESCO).
2. The World Education Forum, held in Dakar, Senegal from 26 to 28 April 2000.

3. The National Council on Women's Education set up in 1958 under the chairmanship of Smt. Durgabai Deshmukh recommended certain specific steps to expand and improve the education of women in the country.

REFERENCES

Agarwal, S.P. (2001), Women's Education in India (1995-98).

Aggarwal, Yash (1995), Recent Trends in Literacy among Scheduled Castes, Occasional paper No. 20, NIEPA, New Delhi.

Aggarwal, Yash and Kusum K. Premi (1998) Reforming School Education: Issues in Policy Planning and Implementation, Vikas Publishers, New Delhi.

Aggarwal, Yash (1988), Education and Human Resource Development, Commonwealth, New Delhi.

Banerji, Rukmini (1997); Why Don't Children Complete Primary School? A Case Study of Low Income Neighborhood in Delhi, EPW, August 9, 1997.

Government of India (1986), National Policy on Education, 1986. MHRD, New Delhi.

Government of India, Census of India 2011.

Gupta, N.L. (2003), Women's Education through Ages, Concept Publications Co, New Delhi.

King, K., Mc Grath, S. & Rose, P. (2007); Beyond the basics: Educating and training out of poverty. International Journal of Educational Development, 27, 349-357.

NCERT (1992). School Education in the 1990s: Problems and Perspectives. Report of the National Seminar, NCERT, New Delhi.

Rao, R.K. (2001). Women and Education, Kalpaz Publications, Delhi.

Robeyns, I. (2005). The capability approach: a theoretical survey. Journal of Human Development, 6, 93-114.

Samuel Ravi, S (2016), A Compressive study of Education, PHI Learning Private Limited, Delhi.

Sharma, Arvind (Ed) (2002), Women in Indian Religions, Oxford University Press.

Sharma, R. (1998), Universal Elementary Education: The Question of How? EPW, Vol. 33(26).

Shukla, S. (1994), Attainment of Primary School Children in India, NCERT, New Delhi.

Walker, M. & Unterhalter, E. (2007), Amartya Sen's capability approach and social justice in education. New York, Palgrave Macmillan.

Web portal; School & Mass Education, Govt.of Odisha.

World Bank (1997). Primary Education in India, Development in Practice Series, World Bank, Washington.

2

Community Based Management of Natural Resources

INTRODUCTION

Community Based Natural Resource Management (CBNRM) is the combined management of natural resources by a community based on a community strategy through a participatory mechanism involving all legitimate stakeholders. The approach is community-based because the communities manage the resources as their legal rights, the local institutions and the economic incentives to take substantial responsibility for sustained use of these resources. This implies that the community plays a dynamic role in the management of natural resources, not because it affirms sole ownership over them, but because it can claim participation in their management and benefits for realistic and technical reasons. This approach emerged as the dominant conservation concept in the late 1970s and early 1980s of the disenchantment with the developmental state.

Rural poor people are not just 'the poor'; they have faces and names. They are real people – poor farmers, poor fishermen, poor nomads and poor women producers and so on. Overcoming poverty means individual and collective empowerment, strengthening productive and income generating capacities and increasing opportunities. This requires a clear understanding of the activities of poor people and of the natural, social, economic and political environment in which they live on. It also requires supportive policies, institutions, services and investment.The last two decades have witnessed a paradigm shift in conservation and natural resource management away from costly state-centered control towards approaches in which local people play a much more active role. These reforms purportedly aim to increase resource user participation in natural resource management decisions and benefits by restructuring the power relations between state and communities through the transfer of management authority to local-level organizations.

A research study was undertaken by Jamir, 2014 in Mokokchung district in Nagaland India on Shifting cultivation, changes and challenges in land-use and livelihoods. Similarly, another study was undertaken by Sharma, Bhuchar, Xing and Kothyari, 2007 on "Land use change and its impact on hydro-ecological linkages in Himalayan watersheds". The study reveals that the land use change is happening in an unprecedented manner in the Himalaya. The natural forest decreased in both the countries with the highest change of 20 percent in Mamlay Watershed of India during 1988 to 1997 and simultaneously the area under open forests increased in most cases. In the Indian watersheds the agricultural land increased with the highest value of 16 percent recorded in the Mamlay watershed over a decade.

To capture forest degradation and rehabilitation of degraded forests the Government of India issued guidelines on June 1, 1990 regarding Joint Forest Management (JFM) stating that JFM programme should be implemented on an arrangement among voluntary agencies, the village community and the forest department. Thus, JFM is one of the recognized organizational systems to regenerate forest resources, meeting local needs of people and sharing expected benefits. Under the system, the local user communities are responsible for the control, protection and management of the forests. Joint forest management advocates strong community participation, bottom up planning and sustainable use of forest resources. Women are also the active users and members of most of the community forests.

Existing work reveals systems of water management, methods of gathering firewood and fodder, and practices of shifting agriculture that were typically not destructive of nature. Some traditional religious and folk beliefs also contributed to the preservation of nature, especially trees or orchards deemed sacred (Gadgil & Vartak, 1975).

According to Bromley & Cernea,1989 note, "the appearance of environmental management created through the establishment of government agencies, and the aura of coherent policy by issuance of decrees prohibiting entry to and harvesting from state property has led to continued degradation of resources under the tolerant eye of government agencies" (1989). CBNRM practices were adopted in several ways through programmes in individual sectors like forestry, irrigation, etc. or multi-sectoral programmes such as watershed development or rural livelihood development. The earlier notion of a state driven development has undergone a change on being replaced by the new strategy of communitarian and civil society driven development.

According to Leach, Mearns, and Scoones,1997 "Community based natural resource management frequently present 'communities' as consensual units, able to act collectively in restoring population resource imbalances or re-establishing harmonious relations between local livelihoods and stable environments."

In the late 1970s and the early decades of 1980s a host of

CBNRM experiments were initiated across the different countries of South Asia and rest of the world that provided the inspiration for subsequent efforts. These early efforts came out as a result of the disillusionment with the developmental state challenged the authority of the state and demanded a space and a voice in decision making for local communities (Kothari, 1989).

There are some ideas of CBNRM and community-based development in general. The first idea is that community-based development is framed in the context of wider hegemonic discourses and practices of development. This critique is grounded in the Foucauldian idea of development as a discursive formation, i.e., practices and perceptions of development are rooted in forms of rationality that allow for a limited form of agency and render 'unthinkable, unsayable and undoable others' (Rossi, 2004). This means that 'alternative' forms of development such as CBNRM could have been and can be constrained by state-centered development and more recently a neo-liberal paradigm of development. Such hegemonic forms of development could limit the extent of devolution to communities, privilege market-based ideologies or make CBNRM a form of what Ferguson has called 'depoliticized' development – all of which could prevent the emergence of new forms of democratization (Ferguson, 1990).

The second idea of some developmental scientists on 'community' in CBNRM are as follows:

(1) communities are often envisaged as communities of shared understanding (Agrawal & Ostrom, 2001; Agrawal & Gibson, 1999) and hence internal differentiations are ignored;

(2) envisaging communities in this manner results in the privileging and marginalizing of certain voices;

(3) the different priorities of the segmented community are not adequately examined, and

(4) communities are imagined as 'autonomous' and in opposition to the state and hence simplified claims are made that community-based management is the definitive solution.

Finally, CBNRM has been analyzed on the 'project mode' in which it has been implemented. Mosse, 2003 and Baviskar, 2004 have highlighted the manner in which targets and achievements often drive the nature of the intervention. There are two dimensions to this project mode resulting in pressure on staff to deliver desirable outcomes and the selection of particular villages for intervention to make outcomes better. Whether or not these constraints are endemic to community-based management requires, as Mosse correctly argues, more ethnographies of development.

OBJECTIVES

The objectives of this paper are to analyze the basic concepts of Natural Resource Management and the significance of Community Based Natural Resource Management. Secondly, the chapter throws light on the relationship of Community Based Natural Resource Management with Poverty, Women, Self Help Groups, devolution of NTFP, Ownership to Panchayats in Odisha. Thirdly, it tries to explain the government initiatives with regard to Community Based Natural Resource Management along with the status, key issues and legal framework of Joint Forest Management in Odisha. Finally, it presents some implications and suggestions for improvement in the Community Based Natural Resource Management.

METHODOLOGY AND SOURCES OF DATA

The methodologies adopted for this chapter are collection of data through the method of Focused Group Discussion (FGD) with help of semi-structured interview to elicit information about the community participation in Natural

Resource Management. The field investigators were advised to stay with the respondents during the data collection to build the rapport with them to explore opportunities to collect the data and information from the field. Furthermore, the information was collected through the Participatory Rural Appraisal (PRA) method. In addition to this, the paper used some data from the secondary sources and present them in final form by reviewing some literatures.

POVERTY AND NATURAL RESOURCE MANAGEMENT

Despite rapid urbanization and increased livelihood diversification, more than sixty percent of India's population still depend on agriculture for their livelihoods. The nexus between poverty and environmental conservation remains strong. Land degradation is a key issue affecting resource productivity. It is estimated that about one third of the soil in India has been affected by erosion. This has a direct impact on agricultural productivity and hence food production, especially for resource poor farmers living off marginal land-holdings. The area declining under forest covered has now been arrested, but the volume and density of forests have been reducing and causing scarcity of valuable forest produce, important for the livelihoods of poor in many regions.

Over exploitation of surface and groundwater threatens the quantity, reliability and quality of water availability. Water is rapidly becoming a scarce resource. Growing scarcity and competition for water poses a major threat to advances in poverty reduction by limiting productive as well as consumptive aspects of livelihoods and well-being. If this trend is not reversed, it is believed that an increasing number of poor people may find more difficulty in securing access to water than securing access to food, primary health care or education. Access to safe water supply and sanitation means lot for economic and social well-being in India.

In many parts of India, low-cost tube well irrigation has stimulated agricultural production for small farmers and brought many households out of poverty. Outside high potential irrigation areas, soil and water conservation alone has increased agricultural productivity and enabled new and additional crops to be grown. It is Watershed Development Programmes in India have largely rested on the assumption that improvements in the resource base would automatically lead to reduction in poverty. One of the biggest challenges of future natural resource management programmes is to contribute to poverty reduction by creating sustainable improvements in the livelihoods of the poor. This will require better targeting and supporting positive directions of change with regard to resource access and equity. Poor people must be included to a greater extent and have a larger say and share in NRM programmes. It has been demonstrated that support to a geographical area with high incidence of poverty or a strategy based on 'poverty inclusion' are inadequate approaches to combat poverty. To understand whether a natural resource development intervention will have desirable livelihood outcomes for the poor requires a framework for poverty analysis. It is generally agreed that poverty is multi-dimensional and dynamic and originates in a set of interlocking factors that reinforce ill-being in individuals, households and communities.

GOVERNMENT INITIATIVES AND COMMUNITY BASED NRM

The effective involvement of local communities in evolving sustainable forest management systems is now being looked upon as an important approach to address the long-standing problems of deforestation and land degradation in India. The National Forest Policy (1988) and JFM Guidelines (1990) of the Government of India have acknowledged and endorsed this system of management, which supports the involvement of village communities and Non-Governmental

Organizations (NGOs) in the management and protection of degraded forests.

For effective planning and management of natural resources, Government of India launched several programmes on watershed basis during various plan periods, through two nodal ministries, MoA and the Ministry of Rural Development – the Department of Land Resources (DoLR). The first such scheme was the 'River Valley Projects (RVP)', launched in 1962-63 by the MoA, followed by the 'Flood Prone Rivers (FPR)' scheme in 1980-81 for integrated watershed management in the catchments of flood-prone rivers.

The National Watershed Development Programme for Rainfed Areas (NWDPRA) was launched in 1990 by the MoA. Simultaneously, the MoA implemented the Watershed Development Programme for Shifting Cultivation Areas (WDPSCA) scheme in the states affected by shifting cultivation. However, to make the watershed management schemes participatory and ensure sustainability and equity, the NWDPRA guidelines were revised to Warasa-Jan Sahabhagita Guidelines. Since April 2013, all the watershed management programmes of the MoA, i.e. RVP, FPR, NWDPRA, WDPSCA and other schemes have been included under one umbrella called Macro Management of Agriculture (MMA).

The other nodal department, i.e. DoLR has implemented three major programmes of watershed management, viz. Drought Prone Areas Programme (DPAP), Desert Development Programme (DDP) and Integrated Wasteland Development Programme (IWDP). The DPAP was launched during 1972-73. The DDP was started in 1977-78 as a special programme for hot desert areas of Rajasthan, Gujarat, Haryana, and cold desert areas of Jammu & Kashmir and Himachal Pradesh. However, all the three have been merged to a single programme called Integrated Watershed Management Programme (IWMP) since 2009-10. The main objectives of IWMP are to restore the ecological balance by harnessing, conserving and developing degraded natural resources such as soil, vegetation cover and water. This enables multi-cropping and the introduction of diverse agro-based activities which help providing sustainable livelihoods to the people residing in the watershed areas.

WOMEN AND SELF HELP GROUPS AS KEY STAKEHOLDERS IN COMMUNITY BASED NRM

Community Based NRM practices seems to be based on at least four major assumptions:

(a) local communities are homogeneous and share both common space and understanding;

(b) Traditionally demarcated domain of work and 'natural' and contributed to resource conservation;

(c) Decentralization ensures efficient resource management; and

(d) Participation and self help are the keys to equitable and sustainable resource use.

If community management is to be community derived rather than community based than its content direction and pace would have to be shaped collectively by the subordinate and the dominant groups in the community. The invisibility of women in Natural Resource Management is related to this very slow process of change in perceptions and practices. Women SHGs have been proliferating since then across India not just in micro credit but also in natural resource management. The use of SHG for natural resource management throws out a large number of challenges.

COMMUNITY BASED NRM (COMMUNITY FORESTRY) AND JFM IN ODISHA

Though Odisha is vibrant in natural resources, it is one of the poorest states in India, in terms of per capita income. The linkages between people and forests are economic as well as cultural. It is common to find villagers depending on forests not only for fuel wood and fodder, but also for income through sale of NTFPs, for wood to repair houses and construct agricultural implements, for shrubs to fence fields and for food. In socio-cultural and economic milieu, Odisha has a long history as well as a large number of self-initiated community-based forest protection and management. High forest dependence, scarcity due to forest degradation, existence of traditional community institutions, and high prevalence of forests within the revenue boundary of villages are often cited as factors that have facilitated initiation and spread of community-based forest management efforts.

Odisha formulated the first formal resolution on involvement of local communities for protection of natural forests in 1988. The state government came out with new JFM resolutions in 1993 and 1996. The 1993 resolution defined the institutional framework for JFM. The 1996 resolution attempted to consolidate the framework by providing for conversion of forests protected by villagers as 'Village Forest', and providing exclusive rights to the members of the Vana Samrakshana Samiti (VSS) on collection and marketing of non-nationalised NTFPs. Above all, the existing framework is seen to create an unequal partnership, which is perceived to be heavily biased in favor of the forest department leading to apprehension that the community would lose the management control they presently exercise over the forest. While the VSS has been made accountable to the forest department for their activities, there is little for the community to ensure the same from FD for its decisions and actions.

So far as the key issues and legal framework of Community Forestry/JFM Policy are concerned, it may be stated that the diverse conditions under which community forest linkages develop and exist reveals the need for a policy and institutional framework that recognize diversity. In places such as Odisha where the initiative for forest protection by communities precedes introduction of JFM, the need for a framework that provides greater control and power to the community organizations is significant. Despite adoption of JFM resolutions, there have been few corresponding changes in the legal framework for forest management. The existing rules and regulations related to forest protection and management needs to be rationalized to provide space and scope for village-based strategies. Local institutions are delegated the management responsibility only through administrative orders. The issue of authority vis-à-vis Panchayats also needs to be resolved, particularly for forests that are located within the village boundary. Currently, under a Supreme Court ruling, no forest area can be worked unless it is covered by a management plan duly approved by the Government of India.

COMMUNITY BASED NRM AND DEVOLUTION OF NTFP OWNERSHIP TO PANCHAYATS IN ODISHA

Under the 73rd Amendment to the Indian Constitution, the Panchayati Raj Institutions (PRIs) have been given the power to manage natural resources including forests. They have also been given ownership of NTFPs. While the exact nature and extent of Panchayat control over NTFPs still needs to be worked out, the policy shift has significant implications for JFM in the state. Although it has created opportunities for local communities to exercise greater control over natural resources and their extraction, at the same time it has created possibilities of conflict between JFM/self-initiated community institutions and PRIs. In the past, similar government resolutions on the issue were defeated by taking out commercially attractive NTFPs by declaring them as major forest produce instead. Apart from this, the ground reality is likely to change unless the primary collectors and the PRIs as well as community institutions are strengthened to carry out their mandated responsibility in a collaborative manner. At various places in Odisha confederations of village organizations involved in forest management have emerged. Such federations are organized at various levels, including district, blocks and Gram Panchayat.

The critical factors seem to be responsible for the success of the CBNRM projects are:

i) Community formation;
ii) Community bonding and networking;
iii) Institutional reforms to accommodate community involvement in the NRM projects;
iv) Institutionalization of NGO participation in the programmes as a catalyst;
v) Government's positive role in engendering partnerships and ensuring fruitful participation of the community.

The creation of an enabling policy environment at central government level which would involve the local communities in biodiversity management is one of the key factors. However, as the cases discussed above also bring to the fore another important factor supportive in the successful operation of CBNRM projects in India, the uniqueness of each situation and the presence of certain situational factors that operate in a positive or a negative way.

Ecology, environment and poverty are closely interwoven and inversely related. Ecological degradation is accompanied by erosion both in the quality and in substance of life of the community living within the eco-space. An ecologically vibrant environment maximizes productive potential of the community leading to livelihood security and income stability.

The task of agricultural development through community-based natural resource management is so complex and formidable that it needs imaginative and concerted effort and well designed thrust. The degree of success in tribal development depends upon the extent to which the tribals are involved in the formulation and implementation of the programs. If the community could be involved directly in the process of development, it will have the desired impact.

IMPLICATIONS AND SUGGESTIONS

For effective planning and efficient implementation of NRM programme both government and NGO can undertake programme on collaborative and co-operation basis. While execution, the implementing agency has to be considered as the clientele felt-needs and their characteristics, which will enhance participation and adoption of NRM technologies ultimately leads to sustainable development.

As per the NRM research, there should be an established network and coordination among the public-funded research organizations cutting across the various departments and ministries engaged in NRM research. The network should be mandatory for the research organizations so that mutual data transfer and multidisciplinary investigations can be possible without unnecessary repetition.

Regular monitoring and appraisal of natural resources is essential to devise appropriate planning. The land degradation statistics is reported by various agencies with different figures by adopting different methodologies and monitoring is not done at regular periodicity. It is essential to develop a sound methodology using the conventional and the remotely sensed data by involving NRSC, ICAR, Wasteland Development Board and the other user agencies in a common platform and develop a framework for monitoring at a fixed time interval.

However, most of the estimates on land degradation report based on the degraded and wasteland statistics, no report is available on the status of soil quality, at least for crop production. The depletion in soil quality is a type of hidden hunger to agricultural growth and may not be visible to be classified as a degraded land until soil becomes fully exhausted. The efforts required to bring back a depleted soil is much higher than those for a depleting soil. Thus, there should be an effort to develop soil quality indices and monitor the soil quality at regular intervals to plan appropriate land-use measures that ensure maintaining soil productivity and allow the soil to optimum soil functions and providing ecosystem services.

For effective planning and implementation of NRM project, the following strategies are worth considering:

- Consistent and effective policies are needed for the protection, conservation and maintenance of soil and water resources.
- Development of NRM technologies that are technically and environmentally sound, economically viable, socially and culturally acceptable and which may lead to sustainable land use.
- Inculcating awareness of land degradation and encouraging adoption of technologies through the use of different media and extension teaching methods.
- Establishment and strengthening of linkages among researchers, extensionists and farmers for effective and efficient transfer of technologies.
- Apart from creating an enabling legal environment, there is the need to support and strengthen the JFM committees and self-initiated community efforts by helping them to become equitable and democratic institutions, which can manage the forest to cater to their various forest-based needs.
- Changes in the community adopted management system are essential to make them more inclusive, equitable,

representative, accountable and transparent. The effectiveness of developing parallel institutions to Panchayat in the form of JFM committees also needs to be considered.

- The lack of knowledge of NRM programme beneficiaries is a constraint in programme planning and implementation and hence it needs awareness generation by using different media and other IEC activities.

REFERENCES

Agrawal, A., & Gibson, C.C. (1999), Enchantment and disenchantment: The role of community in natural resource conservation. World Development, 27(4), 629-649.

Agrawal, A., & Ostrom, E. (2001), Collective action, property rights, and decentralization in resource use in India and Nepal. Politics & Society, 29(4), 485-514.

Amba Jamir's study (2014) on Shifting cultivation, changes and challenges in land-use and livelihoods in Mokokchung district in Nagaland, India.

Baviskar, A. (2004), Between micro-politics and administrative imperatives: Decentralisation and the watershed mission in Madhya Pradesh, India. European Journal of Development Research, Spring, 16 (1), 26-40.

Daniel, W. Bromley, Michael M. Cernea (1989) "Management of Common Property and Natural Resources" published by World Bank Publications, United States; ISBN 10: 0821312499.

Ferguson, James, 1990, The Anti-politics Machine: "Development", Depoliticization, and Bureaucratic Power in Lesotho, University of Minnesota Press, Minneapolis.

Gadgil, Madhav; Vartak, V. D. (1975) Sacred groves of India: A plea for continued conservation Journal of the Bombay Natural History Society, 72 (2). pp. 314-320. ISSN 0006-6982.

Kothari, Rajni, 1989, Politics and People: In Search of a Humane India, Ajanta Publications, Delhi; pp. 24-67.

Leach, M., Mearns R., and Scoones I. (1997), Challenges to community-based sustainable development: Dynamics, Entitlements, Institutions. IDS Bulletin 28(4), 4-14.

Mosse, David, 2003, "Good Policy is Unimplementable? Reflections on the Ethnography of Aid Policy and Practice," in Order and Disjuncture: The Organisation of Aid and Development, SOAS, London; p-1-35.

Rossi, Benedetta, 2004, "Revisiting Foucauldian Approaches: Power Dynamics in Development Projects," The Journal of Development Studies, August 2004, 40(6): 1-29.

Sharma, E & S. Bhuchar, Ma Xing and B.P. Kothyari's study (2007) on "Land use change and its impact on hydro-ecological linkages in Himalayan watersheds".

3

Socio-Economic Development through Rural Development Programmes in India

INTRODUCTION

Development of rural area is the ethos of addressing the veritable needs of the people in the lower crust of the society; rural development signifies a complex and long-term process involving fundamental transformation of rural society both at social and economic levels. It represents planned programmes to improve the quality of the life of the realities. Rural development ameliorates the economic conditions of people and brings a greater transformation of people. In order to provide the rural people with the best prospects, it is imperative to increase participation of the people in the process of rural development programmes, decentralization of planning, better enforcement of land reforms and greater access to credit.

In the post-independent development prospective, the planners and policy-makers hold the view that the state would provide the guiding role in formulating and implementing an enabling policy for poverty alleviation. But it has been experienced that the improvement in living conditions of people cannot be brought about merely from the outside organizational arrangement but by the people's participation in the development process. Therefore, the people centric and people controlled development approach becomes an alternative. It has been unanimously realized that for attainment of progress, it must be based on small locally based and sustainable initiatives to effectively address the issues of sustainability and equity.

Rural development as a strategy has evolved to improve the economic and social well-being of rural people. The term "rural development", in its broad aspect connotes overall development of rural areas to improve the quality of life of rural people. In this sense, it is a comprehensive and multi-dimensional concept, which includes the development of agriculture related activities, village and cottage industries and crafts, socio-economic infrastructure, community services and facilities and above all, human resources in rural areas.

The dictum of rural development has altered considerably during the last three decades. Before seventies, the concept of rural development was aligned with agricultural development and hence focused was on increasing agricultural production. The thrust in this context was primarily to accelerate the pace of rapid industrialization. The perception now goes beyond the improvements in growth, income and output. The concern include an assessment of changes in the quality of life, improvement in health and nutrition, education, environmentally safe living conditions and reduction in gender and income disparity.

Rural pockets are entirely different from the ambit of urban areas. Most of urban people throw their remaining food into the dustbin but in rural and specifically in tribal pockets people do not have food to eat, their conditions are very miserable. Rural people lack in many aspects of a modern living such as education, electricity, infrastructure, health etc. Nearly, seventy percent of the India's population lives in the rural areas. Most of the rural people are reeling in the veil of poverty, illiteracy, unemployment, exploitation, poor health condition, inequitable distribution of wealth and so on.

AIMS AND OBJECTIVES OF RURAL DEVELOPMENT

The prime objectives of rural development are the providing adequate employment opportunities, reduction of under-employment, improve in the standard of living, hygienic living conditions, ensuring quality education, suitable health facility to all, proper sanitation, availability of safe drinking water, well connectivity and converting infrastructural facilities to sustainable livelihood etc. The basic objectives of rural development programme have been alleviation of poverty and unemployment through creation of basic social and economic infrastructure, training for up gradation of skill to the rural unemployed youth and to provide employment to marginal farmers/labourers, so as to discourage seasonal and permanent migration to urban areas. Rural development also includes strengthening the democratic fabric of society through local level governments/institutions and provides the vast rural multitude 'voice and choice' apart from measures to improve rural infrastructure, improve income of rural households and delivery systems pertaining to education, health and safety net mechanism. Poverty alleviation is a key component of rural development.

The salient features of rural development are:

- Raising the standard of living of people in rural areas,
- Alleviating poverty in rural areas and improving the quality of life of the people,
- Development of both farming and non-farming activities so as to generate gainful employment,
- Changing the attitudes of the rural people towards transformation of village community,

- Provision of social infrastructure such as drinking water, health-care, education, sanitation, housing, road, electrification, etc.
- Optimum utilization of local resources without adversely affecting the environment.
- To improve productivity and there by the ensuring assured income of the rural poor.
- To fulfill these aspirations, commitment and willingness for development is essential. A strong commitment to rural development policies at the national level is required for an effective implementation of the wide-ranging programmes of rural development at micro-level.

DEVELOPMENTAL DIFFICULTIES OF RURAL PEOPLE

- The development policy of British administration aimed at revenue collection and their policies were not concerned with the rural development.
- They introduced the Zamindari system to collect as much revenue as they could from the peasants and left peasants most vulnerable. They did very little to improve the condition of the village.
- Britishers extracted minerals from rural land to make Britain economically vibrant. They usually ignored for the upliftment of rural farmers and their land but only exploited its resources.
- Even now people live in the villages without electricity, poor communication, improper roads and other infrastructure development in villages, lack of quality education and quality primary health care and so on
- Many rural people still use the primitive method of cooking, living, using indigenous method of health practices and using labour intensive techniques in agriculture and so on.

- Most of the people in rural area are unemployed. Under employment and even disguised unemployment still persist that lead to under fed, starvation, lack of ability to work, low income and again falling in the vicious circle of poverty.
- Lack of universal quality education, low retention rate, transition rate, low completion rate, migration, siblings care and not ensuring teacher's rationalization, non-adoption of mother tongue based multi lingual education method of teaching learning process. The intensity of rural poverty is seriously aggravating in India.
- The climate change also affects the rural poor adversely as they reside in geographically and environmentally marginal environment with poor infrastructure.
- Even erratic change in temperature as well as extreme weather with floods and droughts adversely affect more the livelihoods of the rural poor.
- Plans, policies, programmes, schemes that have been devised for the betterment of rural people has not been implemented properly, as people do not own and actively participate in the same.
- The most important one, the new generation is migrating to urban areas from the rural areas even government has been launching different programme like Provision of Urban Amenities to Rural Areas (PURA) and Shyama Prasad Mukherji Rurban Mission (SPMRM) or National Rurban Mission in rural area to provide urban amenities to the rural people.
- The financial, manpower, managerial resources devoted to the implementation of rural development programmes are utterly inadequate.
- It has been observed that the objectives of one programme conflict with those of others, and there is no institutional mechanism for rationalizing these programmes.

Consequently, many programmes have utterly failed in fulfilling their objectives.

- In many cases, instruments of rural development are not properly selected, and their levels are not consistent with the objectives they seek to achieve. This results in the wastage of valuable public resources, and unnecessary delay in achieving the objectives.
- The aspect of development, i.e., honesty, hard work, helping others, thrift and such other virtues indirectly help in the economic development and to which much attention has not been paid.
- The political parties who plays very vital role in developing the rural areas are guided more by their own interests at the cost of national interests.
- Even the rural entrepreneurs face typical problems like illiteracy, fear of risk, lack of training and experience, limited purchasing power and competition from the urban entrepreneurs. There are some major problems which are faced by the rural entrepreneurs such as:

  Scarcity of funds: Entrepreneurs fail to get external funds due to the absence of tangible security and the credit facility in the market. The procedure to avail the loan facility is time consuming and that delay disappoints the rural entrepreneurs, which lead to paucity of funds. Therefore, they do not have such financial resources and the external supports to lead their business.

  Competition: Rural entrepreneurs face problems due to the large sized organizations and from the urban entrepreneurs who have different types of products to sell.

  Intermediaries: Rural entrepreneurs, heavily dependent on the middlemen for marketing of their products who garner large amount of profits. They mainly exploit the rural entrepreneurs.

  Legal Procedure: Due to illiteracy and ignorance, rural

entrepreneurs find it extremely difficult in complying with various legal formalities in obtaining licenses.

Procurement of raw materials: Procurement of raw materials is really a tough task for the rural entrepreneurs. They may end up with poor quality raw materials, face problem of storage and warehousing. Due to poor quality of raw materials, they are impelled to make inferior quality of products.

Lacks of technical know: It has Rural entrepreneurs do not have training facilities and extensive services for which they suffer a problem of lack of technical knowledge which impedes for the development.

Negative attitude: The environment of rural families, societies and support system is not conducive to encourage rural people to take up entrepreneurs as a career because of a lack of awareness and knowledge in entrepreneurial opportunities.

Therefore, State intervention to remove of all these barriers can accelerate the process of rural development in India.

DECENTRALIZATION AND DEVELOPMENT

Harmonious blend of decentralization and development can achieve the cherished objectives. Through developmental activities, local accountability, transparency, good governance and citizen participation can be promoted. The most philosophy of development is to establish a balanced and welfare oriented society, equity sharing, economic prosperity, attitudinal changes etc. Decentralization and development are vital in urban areas because they provide citizens to lead social, economic and civic life in a better manner. To accomplish the objectives of rural development, the government should discharge their responsibilities in, allocation of fund, providing financial stability and enhancing public participation.

DEMOCRATIZING DEVELOPMENT

The South African experience shows that democracy cannot guarantee the elimination of poverty and inequality from the economy, but the democratic institutions and an appropriate and conducive political environment may provide the means to address the inequality that prevailed in the society. Therefore, it can be affirmed that democratic politics of socio-economic rights democratizes development and can develop democracy.

A democratic political system does not necessarily guarantee the prevalence of economic development. Moreover, a country that required economic development may not necessarily prioritize democracy too. Therefore, there is a need to a convergence between 'democracy' and 'development'. The following aspects may be considered to inculcate the concept of democratizing development:

- Both democracy and development refer to cumulative processes of social change. Democracy has not guaranteed economic prosperity in recent times.
- Social development provides the key point of intersection between the discourses of democratization and economic development. Social policies and citizenship entitlements will move from the margins to the centre if these two discourses converge.
- If democracy is interpreted as merely holding competitive elections it will have little impact on social development.
- If economic development is seen merely in terms of economic growth then it may favour the choice of an authoritarian regime over a democratic one with little concern for civil or human rights, as has happened in recent history.
- In nineteenth century, democracy and development were seen as more 'intimately' and positively related, with phrases such as 'participation', 'civil society' and

'empowerment' becoming prominent in development literature.

- Through the process of democratizing development, the impact for the rural development can be assessed if development assistance carries democratic conditionality.

EVOLUTION OF RURAL DEVELOPMENT PROCESS IN INDIA

The evolution of rural development in India can be analyzed in pre and post independence periods;

- During pre-independence periods, Britishers were no way concerned about the socio-economic development of India and thus our rural economy was in shambles. The primary concern during that period was their stringent administration for maintenance of law and order and collection of revenue, not the development. Thus, colonial interests were primary objectives and the rural development was at secondary.
- The recurrent famines forced the state administrators to seize the food grains and to distribute among the famine-afflicted people. This was undertaken without any apparent legal sanction, and such the action purely motivated by determination to control profiteering and alleviate rural suffering.
- Removal of barter system and introduction of cash economy by Britishers enabled the peasants to adopt commercial crops. In this way, agricultural subsistence gave rise to commercial crops.
- During the British period, the government adopted several measures such as provision of irrigation facilities, setting up of cooperative societies, creation of a research committee for the comprehension of problems in agriculture etc to combat the agriculture crisis.

During these periods, different types of rural development

models or projects were introduced to reduce the rural poverty which are as follows:

- **Sriniketan Model of Rural Development:** Attempt for rural development was initiated by Rabindranath Tagore in 1908 by establishing youth organization in the Kaligram Pargana of his Zamindari. He tried to create a class of functionary workers who could learn to identify themselves with the people. This was a very comprehensive programme combining culture, health, education and economic aspects of village life together.
- **Martandam Model of Rural Development:** The aim of this project was to bring prosperous life to the rural people. It was intended to symbolize the three-fold development, not only spiritual, mental and physical but also economic and social.
- **Gurgaon Model of Rural Development:** It was started by F.L. Brayne, Deputy Commissioner in the Gurgaon district of Haryana state prompted by backwardness, poverty and misery of the people. Introduction of this programme has improved seeds, implements, the methods of cultivation, etc. This project could not develop leadership in the villages that would continue working when the village guides had left the villages.
- **Sewagram/Gandhian Constructive Model of Rural Development:** The vision of the Gandhiji was to convert the village as self-sufficient and self-radiant. He wanted to remove the developmental problems without any outside interventions and to solve these problems with local people and through local resources. Therefore, for the betterment of people he formulated 18 programmes, love for the mother tongue, economic equality, organization of kisans, labour and students and so on. He gave special attention to revive crafts, especially spinning and weaving, traditional oil press, grain processing and leather work and khadi and village industries with

unflinching faith in the Panchayati Raj and Sahakari Samaj Movement.

- **Rural Reconstruction Programmes in Baroda:** The Maharaja of Baroda was a progressive and enlightened person and therefore he started the Baroda experiment in 1932. This programme aimed at developing "will to live better" and a capacity for the self-help and self-reliance.
- **Rural Development through Firka Development scheme:** The Firka Development scheme of Madras was a government sponsored scheme in 1946. This programme aimed at organizing the villages for a peaceful and more prosperous and fuller life in which the individual villagers had the opportunity to develop both as an individual as well as unit of a well-integrated society.

Similarly, in the post-independence era, the development of rural areas could be accelerated through various flagship programmes and schemes launched by the government–

- The country adopted the planned development from the very first five-year plan by giving importance to agricultural development. It took a number of measures to bring more land under irrigation. Major irrigation Dams like Bhakra Nangal, Hirakud, Nagarjunasagar, Tungabhadra were constructed which generated power for industrialization of the country and water for the irrigation potential.
- Farm mechanization and intensive cultivation of land are very positive developmental step of the government. Farmers were also using the capital-intensive technique in agriculture. They used threshing machines, deep boring and irrigation pumps, which resulted in high yielding improved seeds, fertilizers and other inputs. To procure the same the rural credit system has revitalized with the cooperatives, regional rural banks, and rural branches of commercial banks. In recent time the poor Indian peasants

were also availing the financial support through micro finance system and self-help groups.

- Introduction of land reform including the abolition of the Zamindari system, the abolition of bonded labour system, land ceiling legislation, etc. also accelerated the pace of rural development in India.

Three important projects/programmes for rural reconstruction were introduced just after independence–

- In the year 1948, Albert Mayor started the Etawah Pilot Project for the development of the rural areas in Etawah district in Uttar Pradesh. The main objective of this project was "to see what degree of productive and social improvement as well as initiative, self-confidence and co-operation can be developed.
- In 1948 K.Dey, the former Minister for Community Development and Co-operation was started the Nilokheri experiment, when nearly 7,000 displaced persons were rehabilitated in the Nilokheri town after the independence. The main activities under this programme were a vocational training centre run on co-operative lines and the colony had its own dairy, poultry, piggery, printing press, engineering workshops, tannery and bone-meal factory. People were provided vocational training of their choice to run these co-operative enterprises.
- To create the right atmosphere for the progressive land reforms the Bhoodan Movement was started to prevent the emergence of sanguinary revolution by solving the land problems in a peaceful manner.

GOVERNMENT INITIATIVES FOR RURAL DEVELOPMENT

"If villages prosper the country will prosper, if villages sink the country will sink"; this statement of Gandhiji signified development of village as a precursor to develop mother India. Poverty and unemployment are two inseparable and insuperable problems that India has been facing since the inception of "India that is Bharat". Department of Rural Development has implemented a number of ameliorative programmes in the rural areas through the State Governments for poverty reduction, employment generation, rural infrastructure habitat development, provision of basic minimum services. The Community Development Programme was the first organized attempt for the rural development. The programme was launched on 2nd October in 1952 focusing on all round development of rural areas and upliftment the conditions of rural poor in the field of agriculture, animal husbandry, roads, communication facilities, health, education, housing, employment and nutrition. This is presented in the following table:

Rural Development through	Importance given to	Implemented through Programmes
Multi-Purpose Approach	All round development of villages based on self-help and self-reliance	Community Development Programme (1952)
Sectoral Approach	Intensive development of selected sectors namely, agriculture with concentration in area of comparative advantage	Intensive Agricultural District Programme (IADP) (1960)
Target Approach	Growth with social justice for promotion of weaker section of rural area	Small Farmers Development Agency (SFDA), Marginal Farmers Development Agency (MFDA), Antyodaya (1971)

contd...

Rural Development through	Importance given to	Implemented through Programmes
Area Development Approach	Spatial planning and reduction of regional imbalance	Command Area Development Programme (CADP) (1974)
Basic Needs Approach	Equalisation of social consumption	Minimum Needs Programme (MNP) (1972)
Employment Oriented Integrated Rural Development	Removal of unemployment, poverty through sectoral and area integration	Integrated Rural Development Programme TRYSEM, (1979) DWCRA, Jawahar Rozgar Yojana, (1989) Indira Awas Yojana, Employment Assurance Scheme (EAS), SGSY, (1985) DDP, DPAP, (1970) National Rural Employment Assurance (2006)

Some specific rural development programmes of Government of India were as follows:

Pradhan Mantri Gram Sadak Yojana (PMGSY): As rural roads are vital for the economic growth and measure for poverty alleviation in the village, Government has launched a 100 percent centrally sponsored scheme called the Pradhan Mantri Gram Sadak Yojana. The programme seeks to provide connectivity to all unconnected habitations in the rural areas with a population of more than 500 persons through good all-weather roads by the end of the Tenth Plan period.

Swarnajayanti Gram Swarozgar Yojana (SGSY): It is a self-employment programme for the rural poor that came into effect from 01 April, 1999, it has been conceived as a holistic programme covering all aspects of self-employment like organization of rural poor into Self Help Groups (SHGs) and their capacity building, training, planning of activity clusters, infrastructure development, financial assistance through bank credit and subsidy and marketing support etc.

Rural Housing (Indira Awaas Yojana/Pradhan Mantri Awas Yojana-Gramin): Housing is one of the basic requirements for human survival. Therefore, provision of housing was included as one of the major activities under the National Rural Employment Programme which started in 1980. The Government of India, in 1998 announced a National Housing and Habitat policy, which aims at providing "Housing for all" and facilitating the construction of 20 lakh additional housing units (13 lakh in rural areas and 7 in urban areas) with emphasis on providing durable assets to the poor and the deprived. The Action is being implemented through various programmes such as Indira Awaas Yojana (IAY), Credit cum Subsidy Scheme for Rural Housing, Innovative Scheme for Rural Housing and Habitat Development, Rural Building Centers, Equity Contribution by Ministry of Rural Development to HUDCO and National Mission for Rural Housing and Habitat.Now the scheme has been changed to Pradhan Mantri Awas Yojna (PMAY-G)-Rural and Urban. In Odisha also Biju Pucca Ghara Yojna and Nirman Shramik Pucca Ghar Yojna have been implementing for providing benefit to the rural people.

DRDA Schemes: In order to strengthen the DRDAs and to make them more professional and effective, a new centrally sponsored scheme, namely DRDA Administration has been introduced since 1st April, 1999.

Training Schemes: Training is imperative for effective implementation of the rural development activities concerning various poverty alleviation programmes. As training, research and development are closely linked, continuing education of both policy makers and programmers implements is of vital importance. In order to facilitate this, National Institute of Rural Development (NIRD) has conducted training programmes, workshops, seminars and international programme. In addition, extensive support has been provided to a number of training and research institutions dealing with issues related to rural development.

Integrated Rural Development Programme (IRDP): The programme was launched by the Centre in March 1976 as a major instrument of the government to alleviate poverty. Its main feature was to enable selected families to cross the poverty line in a given time-frame by taking up self-employment in various activities like agriculture, horticulture, animal husbandry, weaving and handicrafts and services and business activities.

Food for Work Programme (FWP): The programme was introduced in 1977 by the then Janata government with the objective to provide employment to the unemployed/ underemployed village persons during the lean season. The wages paid to the workers were in kind, i.e., food grains.

National Rural Employment Programme (NREP): This is the redesigned programme of FWP, planned for creating additional employment opportunities in the rural areas with the help of surplus food grains. This programme was especially for those rural people who mostly depended on wage employment, but had no source of income during lean agricultural period. Later on, this programme was merged with Jawahar Rozgar Yojana (JRY).

Rural Landless Employment Guarantee Programme (RLEGP): Special schemes were formulated by some states such as Maharashtra and Gujarat to provide increased employment opportunities for the rural people, especially landless people.

Jawahar Rozgar Yojana (JRY): This programme came into existence in April 1989 with the merger of the NREP and the RLEGP. Under this scheme, it was expected to provide at least one member of each poor family (BPL family) an employment for 50 to 100 days in a year at a work near his/her residence. About 30 per cent of the jobs under this programme was reserved for the women. The scheme was implemented through Village Panchayats.

Antyodaya Yojana: The word 'antyodaya' is a combination of two words– ant meaning end or bottom level and udaya meaning development. Thus, as a whole, it implies the development or welfare of a person standing at the end of that queue (lowest level), that is, the poorest of the poor.

Mahatma Gandhi National Rural Employment Guarantee Scheme (MGNREGS): For the purpose of extending the benefits to rural people, a new scheme was launched and legislation was enacted under the name of 'National Rural Employment Guarantee Act' (NREGA) September, 2005. It guarantees 100 days of employment in a financial year to any rural household whose adult members are willing to do unskilled manual work. The Act came into force initially in 200 districts, and was extended gradually to other areas notified by the Central Government. It is considered as a "Silver Bullet" for eradicating rural poverty and unemployment, by way of generating demand for productive labour force in the Indian village. It provides an alternative source of livelihood which will have an impact on reducing migration, restricting child labour, alleviating poverty, and making villages self-sustaining through the productive assets creation such road construction, cleaning up of water tanks, soil and water conservation work, etc. It has been considered as the largest anti-poverty programme in the world.

The other programmes are implementing by the ministry of Rural Development are Sabki Yojana Sabka Vikas, Rashtriya Gram Swaraj Abhiyan, Mission Antyodaya, DDU-GKY, DAY-NRLM, NSAP, RURBAN (NRuM), SAGY, Swachh Gram and so on.

These programmes along with other programmes and schemes have been implemented by the government for eradication of poverty as well as the development of rural areas. Many non-governmental organizations are also working alongside government for the same purpose. Although the implementation of these programmes has transferred in the life of rural people, but still there is absolute need to promote these programs at a wider level to achieve great success.

IMPLICATIONS AND CONCLUSION

- The villages in Indian sub-continent have been neglected and remained under developed. When every village in the country will be provided with the basic amenities, like drinking water, electricity, health care, education, transport, communication and other facilities, we will certainly enrich the concept of a welfare state and make India progressive and prosperous across the globe.
- When people will empower, they will get their rights and entitlements. Their income will increase. The increased purchasing power of the rural population will command more demand for the goods and services, which will prominently boost the national economy of India. With socio-economic resurgence, we are optimistic the reverse migration of people from the urban slums back to the villages.

- Programme iniated to transform rurla life must be vigorously, honestly as well as patriotcally pursued to ensure the sucess of such programme..
- The government has already taken the initiative to improve the condition of the village. The only task left for its better implementation. Together with the government, the people living in rural area should contribute with a great accountability to the process of development. With their contribution and active participation, the country will flourish by way of socio-economic and cultural re-orientation and rejuvenation.
- Adopt institutional arrangements that promote collaboration and cooperation among key agencies and interests; build consensus, educate the public through community level campaign and mobilize local resources.
- Adopt the concept of "Think Globally, Act Locally", which is also the essence of SDG now.
- Emphasize the role of partnership agreement – strengthening business and industry involvement and accountability.
- Promote public participation in the planning and decision-making process with special reference to women and community-based organizations through the information dissemination, education, innovative Information-Education and Communication (IEC) etc.
- The role of governmental and non-governmental organizations for rural development is indeed inevitable.
- A cohesive, collective and concerted effort will be a pragmatic approach that indubitably make India economically vibrant to fulfill the cherished goal of Gandhiji to transform our country with social resurgence and cultural efflorescence.

REFERENCES

Asadi Ali, Akbari Morteza, et. al. (2008) "Poverty Alleviation and Sustainable Development: The Role of Social Capital" Journal of Social Sciences, 4 (3):202-215.

Acharya, Bala Ram, Dimension of Rural Development in Nepal, Dhaulagiri, Journal of Sociology and Anthopology, Vol. 2.

Basu, Pratyush and Chakraborty, Jayajit (2008) Land, Labour and Rural Development: Analyzing Participation in India's Village Dairy Cooperatives; The Professional Geographer, 60 (3) Aug, 299-313.

Bourguignon, F., and C. Morrisson. 1998. "Inequality and Development: The Role of Dualism." Journal of Development Economics 57: 233-258.

Joachin, Braun Von, Gulati, Ashok, Hazell Peter, Rosegrant W. Mark, Ruel Marie (2006) "Indian Agriculture and Rural Development" Strategic Issues and Reform Options.

Chandrasekra, Wijayratna. M. (2002) "Role of Local Communities in Integrated Rural Development".

Clark, J. (1991), Democratizing Development: The role of voluntary Organisation, London: Earthscan.

Das, Purnendu Sekhar (2005): Decentralization Planning and Participatory Rural Development, Concept Publishing Company, New Delhi.

Datt, G. and M. Ravallion.1998a. "Farm Productivity and Rural Poverty in India." Journal of Development Studies, 34 (4): 62-85.

Datt, G. and M. Ravallion.1998b. "Why have some Indian States done better than others at reducing rural poverty?" Economica, 65: 17-38.

Desai, Vasant (1988): Rural Development (Vol. II), Programmes Strategies, Himalaya Publishing House, Bombay.

Desai, Vasant (1988): Rural Development (Vol.1) Issues & Problems, Himalaya Publishing House, Bombay.

Economic and Social Development Department, Reducing Poverty And Hunger: The Critical Role of Financing For Food, Agriculture and Rural Development, Paper Prepared for the International Conference on Financing for Development Monterrey, Mexico, 18-22 March 2002.

Gehlawat, J.K. and Kant K. (1987): Strategies for Rural Development. Arnold Publishers (India) Pvt. Ltd., New Delhi.

Government of India, Planning Commission, First Five Year Plan, New Delhi, pp.223-24 (1952).

Jain, Meenu, Rural Development Programmemes, Department of Economics, D.A.V. College, Yamunanagar, Haryana, Kurukshetra University, Kurukshetra, 1 (2010).

Jain, S.P. (1997) The Gram Sabha: Gateway to Grassroot Democracy, Journal for Rural Develoment, 16 (4), Oct-Dec.

Jelena, Petkovic, Traditional Values And Modernization Challenges In Forming Urban and Rural Culture, Vol. 6, No. 1, 2007, pp. 23-39.

Jha, Raghbendra (2000) "Rural Poverty in India: Structure, determinants and suggestions for policy reform" Journal of Development and Change, 32(2), 45-48.

Kelles-Viitanen, Anita, New Challenges and Opportunities for Rural Development, Paper presented at the IFAD workshop what are Innovation Challenges for Rural Development, in Rome (2005).

Luiz, R. D. Agostini & Alfredo C. Fantini, Quality of Life and Quality of Living Conditions in Rural Areas 89, 487-499 (2008).

Madan, G.R., India's Developing villages, Allied Publishers, New Delhi, 43 (1990).

Mishra, B.B, District Administration and Rural development, Oxford University Press, New Delhi, 1983, p.6.

Myrdal, Gunnar (1957) "Economic Theory and underdeveloped regions", Bombay, Valu and Co. Publishers Pvt. Ltd.

Prasad, K.N., India's Rural Problems, Concept Publishing Company, New Delhi, 1991, p. 254.

Randhawa, M.S., Developing Village India, Orient Longman, Bombay, 39-42 (1951).

Saxena, Sandeep, Problems Faced by Rural Entrepreneurs and Remedies to Solve It, ISSN: 2278-487-X Volume 3, Issue 1 (July-Aug. 2012), pp 23-29.

Sen, A.K., (1999), Development as a Freedom, Oxford U.K., Oxford University Press.

Shriman, Narayan, Towards the Gandhian Plan, S. Chand & Co., New Delhi, 74 (1978).

Singh, Katar (1986) "Rural Development Principles and Policies and Management", Sage Publication, New Delhi.

Vagdevi, H. S. & Deepa T.M, Rural Development: A Holistic Approach, Volume 3, Issue 3, Jul-Sep., 2015.

Vidyarthi, L.P. (Ed), Rural Development in South Asia, Concept Publishing Company, New Delhi, 1982, p.20.

Whitehead, L. 2002, Democratizing Development, United Nations Research Institute for Social Development (UNRISD), working paper, November, 2002.

4

Management of Human Resources and Globalization

INTRODUCTION

Globalisation has opened a new horizon in the field of economy. The world has experienced its effects on different aspects of lives such as economical, social, environmental and political from many years ago. Economic globalization includes flows of goods and services across borders, international capital flows, reduction in tariffs and trade barriers, immigration, and the spread of technology, and knowledge beyond borders. It is source of much debate and conflict like any source of great power.

The rapid renovation in human resources at present is a derivative of the rapid changes in businesses on account of globalization. In the global competition within the flat and connecting new world, decision making in organizations has become increasingly intricate and convoluted. The new global world has widened the talent pool for excellent and marginal workers and for permanent and fluid workers. An organization's talent can be a source for a sustained competitive advantage and can affect important organizational outcomes such as survival, profitability, customer satisfaction level, and employee performance. Human resources need to take advantage of technology and data analytics to build a global human resource information system that collects and stores data from various sources. The system will help to analyze the data to provide business insights, predict future needs and devised strategies to fulfill/address needs.

The global supply of talent is short of its long-term demand, and the gap is a challenge for employers everywhere. The deficiency in the demand and supply of talent is continuously increasing for high skilled workers and for the next generation of business administrators. Most emerging nations with large populations, including Brazil, Russia, India, and China, may not be able to sustain a net surplus workforce with the right skills for much longer. Now, more than ever, organizations need to place greater emphasis on attracting human capital rather than financial capital. Because capital is broadly available from investors and lenders, and innovations can be duplicated relatively easily and quickly. Effective human resource management is the best way to differentiate one company from another. Only the multinationals willing to adapt their human resource practices to the changing global labour market conditions will be able to attract, develop and retain the right talent, and will likely succeed in the global competition.

The relationship between globalization and growth is a highly sensitive and debated topic on the growth and development literature. But, this issue is not yet resolved. Theoretical growth studies report at best a contradictory and inconclusive discussion on the relationship between globalization and growth. Some of the studies found positive effect of globalization on growth through effective allocation of domestic resources, diffusion of technology, improvement in factor productivity and augmentation of capital. In contrast, others argued that globalization has harmful effect on growth in countries with feeble institutions and political instability and in countries, which specialized in ineffective activities in the process of globalization (Samimi & Jenatabadi, 2014).

Dreher, (2006) introduced a 'new comprehensive index of globalization to examine the impact of globalization on growth in an unbalanced dynamic panel of 123 countries between 1970 and 2000. The overall result showed that globalization promotes economic growth. The economic and social dimensions have positive impact on growth whereas political dimension has no effect on growth. The positive effect of globalization on economic growth is also confirmed by the extreme bounds analysis. The result indicated that the positive effect of globalization on growth is larger than the effect of investment on growth.'

The second school of thought, supported by some scholars like Rodriguez and Rodrik (2000) believed that "weak evidence support the idea of positive relationship between openness and growth. They mentioned the lack of control for some prominent growth indicators as well as using incomprehensive trade openness index as shortcomings of these works".

The third school of thoughts (Borensztein, Gregorio & Lee, 1998) found that 'there is non-linear relationship between globalization and growth with emphasis on the effect of complementary policies. Calderón and Poggio (2010) examined "the structural factors that may have impact on growth effect of trade openness. The growth benefits of rising trade openness are conditional on the level of progress in structural areas including education, innovation, infrastructure, institutions, the regulatory framework, and economic development. Indeed, they found that the lack of progress in these areas could restrict the potential benefits of trade openness".

Gu and Dong (2011) emphasized that 'the harmful or useful growth effect of financial globalization heavily depends on the level of financial development of economies. In fact, if financial openness happens without any improvement in the financial system of countries, growth will replace by volatility'.

The objectives of this chapter are to analyze the basic concepts of globalisation and it's impact on human resource management. Here this paper tries to explain the different dimensions of global impact of globalisation on human resource.

The methodologies adopted for this chapter were the analysis of data and information of some research based discussion on globalisation and it's global impact. In addition to this, the paper used some data from the secondary sources and by reviewing some literatures.

The increasing prevalence of globalization is driven by a number of factors, including shortage of talent in developed countries, availability of low cost labour and growing consumers in developing countries and technological progress.

PAUCITY OF GLOBAL BRAINS IN DEVELOPED COUNTRIES

Despite the current economic recession and unemployment, most developed countries, including the United States, Germany and Japan are facing long-term talent shortages. There are more workers retiring than entering the labour force in these countries. By 2020, for every five retiring workers, only four new workers will join the labour force in most developed countries. According to one estimate, the United States will need to add 26 million workers to its talent pool by 2030 to sustain the average economic growth of the two past decades (1988-2008) unless a technological breakthrough replaces manpower, while Western Europe will need to add 46 million employees (World Economic Forum, 2010). The shortage of workers is predicted across most industries, including manufacturing, construction, transport and communications, trade, hotel and restaurants, financial services,

IT and business services, health care, public administration, and education.

ACCESSIBILITY OF LOW PRICED LABOUR IN EMERGING COUNTRIES

The opportunity has never been greater for multinationals to attract top talent from emerging countries, such as Brazil, Russia, India, and China or to outsource work to these countries. Global population growth differs greatly between developed and developing countries. In the developed countries, USA, EU, and Japan, the current annual rate of growth is less than 0.3 percent, while in the rest of the world the population is increasing almost six times as fast. According to McKinsey Global Institute, there are approximately 33 million potential professionals in emerging markets who are growing very quickly. The total number of university-educated workers in low-wage countries far exceeds the number for higher wage countries. Currently, India produces as many young engineers as the United States, and China produces more than twice as many. Russia produces ten times as many finance and accounting professionals as Germany. According to the International Organization for Migration, there were an estimated 214 million international migrants in the world in 2010, and fifty-seven per cent of all migrants live in high-income countries (World Migration Report, 2010). The number of migrants is likely to grow exponentially in the coming years. Furthermore, the migration of workers and outsourcing of work would not be limited to the unidirectional flow from emerging countries to developed countries.

IMPROVEMENT IN TECHNOLOGY

Globalization is made possible by the development of cost effective, yet very powerful technologies, including the Intra and Internet, enterprise resource planning system, data warehouse, data mart, and data analytics. 'Friedman (2005) defined globalization a whole set of technologies and political events converging including the fall of the Berlin Wall, the rise of the internet, the diffusion of the windows operating system, the creation of a global fibre-optic network, and the creation of interoperable software applications, which made it very easy for people all over the world to work together that levelled the playing field. It created a global platform that allowed more people to plug and play, collaborate and compete, share knowledge and share work, on a scale never seen before. Cloud computing and new advances in remote access and support technologies also seem to fuel globalization. Many service jobs, such as call centres, animation, transcription, and software development can be carried out remotely. It is estimated that 160 million jobs, or about 11 percent of the projected 1.46 billion service jobs worldwide in 2008, could be carried out remotely, barring any constraints on supply (McKinley Global Institute, 2005-I)'.

LIMITATIONS OF GLOBALIZATION

It has seen that 'the demand for such talent is likely to grow even faster in the same period. Based on data from 22 countries and 12 industries, a World Economic Forum study predicted that vast talent gaps between the supply and demand of highly skilled workers would appear by 2020 (World Economic Forum, 2011). The demand for talented people is growing not only from developed countries, but from the developing countries themselves as they pursue their own nation building'.

One of the biggest challenges for global organizations that 'manage diverse human resource workforce in culture and language skills and distributed in various countries. It is critical that the businesses not only familiarize with local ways of doing business and understand the needs of local consumers, but also develop a global mindset among their employees. Being at the centre of globalization, multinational organizations need to learn to integrate diverse value systems and espouse shared global work values to create an environment, where workers are able to communicate and coordinate their activities to reach common goals. Human resources must play new roles and responsibilities in leading the organization in uncharted waters of globalization (Rosenblatt, 2011)'.

The increasing incidence of globalization is driven by a number of factors, including shortage of talent in developed countries, availability of low cost labour and growing consumers in developing countries, and technological progress. Despite the current economic downturn and unemployment, most developed countries, including United States, Germany and Japan will face long term talent shortages mainly due to ageing and retirement of baby boomers. There are more workers retiring than entering the labour force in these countries. By 2020, for every five retiring workers, only four new workers will join the labour force in most developed countries. The shrinkage of talent will be more than compensated by growing number of professional talent produced in emerging nations, yet the global supply of talent is short of its long-term demand, and the gap is a challenge for employers everywhere. The shortage between the demand and supply of talents is likely to continue to increase, notably for highly skilled professionals. The demand for talented people is increasing from developed and developing countries alike. Only the multinational enterprises that will be willing to adapt their human resource practices to the changing global labour market conditions will be able to attract, develop and retain high performing employees, and will likely to survive, and succeed in the global competition. Management of culturally diverged and geographically dispersed workforce is a key goal of global human resources. It is also critical that the businesses not only familiarize with local ways of doing business, and understand needs of the local consumers, but also develop a global mindset among their employees. Human resources must play roles and responsibilities in leading the organization towards openness to cultural diversity. Various new technologies have emerged that are helpful for human resource professionals to manage the processes involved in globalization but there are also certain challenges faced by the organizations. The human resource department must recruit and retain talented employees at a global level. Since the company has to deal with changing demands, professionals will have a need to predict and manage culture-fit policies.

With the great impact of globalization, demand for people has increased for highly skilled jobs or positions that require specialized knowledge. It becomes difficult for human resource professionals to locate such people in the nearby areas, they have looked for them globally. HR experts progressively are entrusted with working new computer system frameworks required to deal with a worldwide workforce. Human resource professionals have to spend a considerable time and effort to learn new platforms when their companies rely on the latest software to manage a worldwide workforce.

A major aspect of globalization on HR experts is the necessity to determine and understand the cultural and social dissimilarities at play with their new global manpower. They must know how best to communicate company goals and missions, integrate diverse value systems into their companies and coordinate the activities of all their employees to achieve their goals. With advancement in technology, change in use of technology is also required. It becomes imperative for the organization to use the latest techniques and software. The organizations are tasked with operating new system software. This requires a considerable amount of time and effort to make the employees learn new platforms. Even the employee retention is of great concern for both international and domestic companies.

Actually, internet has made global communication simpler, but time zones have not. HR must devise ways to deliver and communicate vital information in a timely manner. To meet this challenge, Human Resource Department must deliver the emergency information through email alerts or telephonically, so that no communication gap occurs. Certain training programs are supposed to be devised to deliver training to the employees sitting in distant locations. This can be achieved by the virtual training concept, which can be conducted through online videos or tele-conferences.

The other challenge for the companies is 'if they want to send an employee abroad for work purposes, they must make suitable arrangements for him who might even include asking him to develop new language skills'.

The most important thing that needs to be considered by the organizations and a company is to understand and apply the laws of different jurisdictions to a particular organization or company. There are not only tax and labour laws to be considered but also regional and local laws that apply to companies that operate in different states or different countries. Hiring employees at branch locations in different locations might change the requirements on minimum wage, tax allowances or working hours. Understanding and following these laws are vital as it has a great impact on the reputation and working of the company or organization.

CONCLUSION

Globalization permit to increase competition, winch up barriers to entry for developing countries, helps to promote economic growth and facilitate to unify the world's economies. 'The human resources need to focus on organizations long-term objectives and on future-oriented plans. Instead of focusing completely on internal human resource issues, human resource departments need to take a balanced and broader approach. 'Human resource sectors of global companies must accumulate data on factors, such as employees, attrition and hiring, compensation and benefits, ethnic, gender, cultural, and nationality distributions and load into data warehouses and data marts. By applying advanced methodical techniques on the data, human resource professional will get business insight, affirm/profess changes and make informed decisions at operational and strategic levels. The human resource professional accesses current and anticipate future skills shortages through strategic skills planning. Global organizations not only need to a networked, collaborative and open to culturally diverse workforce but also consists of high talent'.

The public policies designed to integrate the world might not optimal for economic growth by itself. Economic globalization not only directly promotes growth but also indirectly catapults by way of complementary reforms.

The policy implications in this context are relatively undemanding. Amalgamating to the global economy is only one part of the story. In this respect, the responsibility of policymakers is to improve the level of educated workers and strength of financial systems to get more opportunities from globalization. These economic policies are important not only in their own right, but also in helping developing countries to derive the benefits of globalization.

Nevertheless, the execution of new technologies transferred from advanced economies requires skilled workers. Indeed, countries with higher level of human capital can better and faster imitate and implement the transferred technologies. The higher level of human capital and certain skill of human capital determine whether technology is successfully absorbed across countries. It shows the importance of human capital in the success of countries in the globalizing world.

The financial openness in the form of FDI brings along the knowledge and managerial ability for implementing the new technology. It can be helpful in promoting the level of human capital in host countries. Moreover, the economic globalization affects growth, whether the effect is beneficial depends on the level of income of countries. High and middle income countries benefit from globalization whereas low-income countries do not desirably gain from it. The structure of the export of low-income countries heavily depends on primary commodity and natural resource which make them susceptible to the global influx.

Globalization builds for a larger labour team from which to choose, but it also increases the possibility of language and cultural barriers in the recruitment process. If the company does not address such barriers, it can make the recruitment process increasingly time-consuming and difficult. Human resource managers must get used to the different customs and cultures at the time hiring employees in different countries. Language barriers also may require hiring bilingual employees and adapting employee documents, such as employee manuals and training materials, into different languages.

With increasing globalization, human resources managers must stay side by side of the labour laws of the countries in which they operate to ensure that the company is not unintentionally breaking these laws. Furthermore, human resource management should make certain that they are not taking advantage of labour laws that may be more slipshod in other countries than those in their native country.

Globalization has a significant effect on the labour force of a company. It allows for more miscellanies within the corporation as well as economic growth for the countries in which the company is hiring. Human resources manager should be conscious about the negative effect that economizing the employee's morale, because the decreased self-esteem often leads to decreased production. Management of human resources should have proactive measures in place that address such morale issues.

REFERENCES

Ates, D. (2005), Economic liberalization and changes in fundamentalism: The case of Egypt. Middle East Policy 12: 133-144.

Belcourt, Monica and Kenneth McBey, Strategic Human Resources Planning, Cengage Learning, 2010

Bhandari, AK, Heshmati, A (2005), Measurement of Globalization and its Variations among Countries, Regions and over Time. IZA Discussion Paper, No.1578.

Birdsall, N (2002), A stormy day on an open field: asymmetry and convergence in the global economy. 66-87.

Borensztein, E, De Gregorio J, Lee JW (1998), How does foreign direct investment affect economic growth? Journal of International Economics, 45: 115-135.

Calderón, C, Poggio V (2010), Trade and Economic Growth Evidence on the Role of Complementarities for CAFTA-DR Countries.

Chang, CP, Lee CC (2010), Globalization and Economic Growth: A Political Economy Analysis for OECD Countries. Global Economic Review 39: 151-173.

Chang, R, Kaltani L, Loayza NV (2009), Openness can be good for growth: The role of policy complementarities. Journal of Development Economics 90: 33-49.

Dreher, A (2006), Does Globalization Affects Growth? Empirical Evidence from a New Index. Applied Economics 6: 1091-1110.

Dreher, A, Gaston N, Martens P (2008), Measuring globalisation: Gauging its consequences: Springer Verlag.

Fischer, S (2003), Globalization and its challenges. American Economic Review, 93:1-30.

Gu, XH, Dong BM (2011), A Theory of Financial Liberalisation: Why are Developing Countries so Reluctant? World Economy 34: 1106-1123.

Hamel, G. and Prahalad, C.K. (1994), Competing for the Future. Boston Mass: Harvard Business School Press.

Harrison, A (1996), Openness and growth: A time-series, Cross-country analysis for developing countries. Journal of Development Economics 48: 419-447.

Hutchinson, S. and Purcell, J. (2003) Bringing policies to life: the vital role of front line managers in people management. Executive Briefing, London: Chartered Institute of Personnel and Development.

Kobrin, S.J. (1988), Expatriate Reduction and Strategic Control in American Multinational Corporations, Human Resource Management, 27.

McGovern, Patrick, Lynda Gratton, Veronica Hope-Hailey, Philip Stiles and Catherine Truss (2007), Human Resource Management on the line? Human Resource Management Journal, Volume 7, Issue 4.

Milliman, J., Von Glinow, M.A. and Nathan, M (1991), Organizational Life Cycles and Strategic International Human Resource Management in Multinational Companies: Implecations for Congruence Theory, Academy of Management Review, 16.

Parisa, Samimi & Hashem Salarzaden Jenatabadi, 2014, "Globalization and Economic Growth: Empirical Evidence on the Role of Complementarities."

Prahalad, C.K. (1983), Developing Strategic Capability: An Agenda for Top Management, Human Resource Management, 22: 237-54.

Rodriguez, F, Rodrik D (2000), Trade policy and economic growth: a skeptic's guide to the cross-national evidence. NBER Macroeconomics Annual, 15: 261-325.

Rosenblatt (2011), "The impact of institutional processes, social networks, and culture on diffusion of global work values in multinational organizations', Cross Cultural Management": An International Journal, Vol. 18, No. 1.

Schuler, R.S. and Jackson, S. (1987), Linking Competitive Strategies with Human Resource Management Practices, Academy of Management Executive, 1.

Tung, R.L. and Punnett, B.J. (1993), The Relationship of Staffing Practices to Organizational Level Measures of Performance, Personnel Psychology, 46: 27-48.

Ulrich, Dave (1996), Human Resource Champions: The next agenda for adding value and delivering results. Boston, Mass: Harvard Business School Press.

World Economic Forum (2010a), Stimulating Economies through Fostering Talent Mobility.

World Economic Forum (2011), Global Talent Risk: Seven Responses.

5

Forest Rights Act and Community Based Forest Management

INTRODUCTION

The relationship between forest and human beings reaches over a long history going back to the evolution of humans on planet earth. In the past, at the time the humans had no knowledge of cultivation, they lived in the forest, depending totally on forest produce for their subsistence. Gradually, early humans learnt to hunt wildlife for food, discovered fire and its use, started eating cooked food, cleared forests for cultivation and communication, constructed huts and developed cultivable land. In course of time, with the development in different fields, human communities cleared more and more forest, constructed means of communication and developed villages and later on towns. With a growing birth rate and a controlled death rate, more and more forest were converted into cultivable lands, roads, homestead lands to meet the needs of the growing population and as a result the forest moved far away from many people living in the towns. However, in a developing country like India, 70 percent of its population lives in rural areas and have still maintained the age-old relationship between humans and the forest. But there are striking changes in the relationship between humans and their natural environment.

Among the rural, certain communities like tribals live in and with the forest. While other people live in the towns far away from the forest with comfortable and luxurious lifestyles, a majority of the tribal's prefer to live in the forest with their own traditional ways of living even today. There are number of such instances in which tribal's, after being displaced and evicted for various reasons, have come back to live in their original homelands. Thus communities, who love to live in the forest, look towards the forest as part of their life and as the main source of their livelihoods and subsistence. They live a simple life, they use the forest to cater to their minimum needs and do minimal harm to the forest. Their lifestyles and use of forest resources are more sustainable in the process of forest management. In this respect, they are different from those communities who have destroyed the forest and left the forest to lead a dignified life, away from the forest.

The main objective of this chapter is to inculcate the idea of a structural changes and shifting in the entire process of forest management and protection from state to community. This paper has explained the degree of success achieved by the community in managing and protecting the forest and the socio-economic benefit they received out of that.

On analysis of the first hand data have been collected from the field along with the data collected from the secondary sources. More specifically the other methods followed are Focused Group Discussion (FGD), collecting case studies, direct personal interview with the stakeholders of this forest rights.

FOREST FROM GOVERNMENT'S PERSPECTIVE

When we analyze the policies and practices adopted by different governments in India, both in pre-independence British Government's period and post independence Indian

Government's period, we can easily conclude the perspective of the government looks at the forest. During the British period, the government looked at the forest as a vast source of timber and it created Forest Department to manage these timbers to earn more revenue. So government did not recognize the symbiotic relationship between the forest and forest dwelling communities and declared forests as national property. As a result, the dense forests in the country were leased out, allowed to be felled and sold. The government not only nationalized forest species (timber) having monetary value but also nationalized many leaves, roots, fruits and flowers. Independent India was continuing the policies of the British Government and did not recognize the relationship between the forest dwelling community and the forest. Remarkable changes occurred in 1970s and 1980s in which Government of India shifted its perspective on the forest from "timber to environment" and "timber to wildlife protection" and so on. However, control and ownership over forest still remained exclusively at the State Forest Department of the government. Ignoring the relationship between the forest and the tribals and other forest dwelling communities and using the same colonial Indian forest Act, 1927, the Government declared large area of forest as Reserved Forest in 1970s, depriving large number of tribals and forest dwellers of their forested homelands. The situation worsened by the government declaring good forest areas as sanctuaries and national parks in 1980s using the provisions of the Wild Life Protection Act, 1972. The 1988 Indian Forest Policy was framed to realize the target of 33 percent of forest cover over the total geographical area and to fulfill the set target of set by the 1988 Forest Policy, Joint Forest Management Resolution was launched in 1990s as an administrative measure to involve the community in the forest protection and management at the village level.

The instrumentation of then Inspector General of Forest

(IGF) on 2nd May, 2002 to the Chief Secretaries of all the State Governments on the direction of the apex court is an important of event in the history of the forest people of the country which denotes that the Supreme Court was seized of the pernicious problem of encroachment of forest lands raised in the Godaverman Thirumulpad vs Union of India case and in response the Supreme Court of India by its order dated 23rd November 2001 restrained the Central Government from regularizing encroachments in the country without its express permission. Based on an inventive interpretation of an arbiter dictum of the Supreme Court, the Inspector General of Forests directed all the State Governments including Odisha to prepare a time bound programme for summary eviction of all encroachments not eligible for regularization through MoEF 1990s guidelines, by 30th September 2002. Emboldened by the dubious letter, which insinuated that the Supreme Court had directed immediate action to evict encroachers, forced evictions of adivasis and forest dwellers took place across the country in a scale unprecedented in recent history. Forest personnel in different States adopted diverse coercive means to drive whole villages out of the forest and destroyed houses of the tribals and forest dwellers resulting forceful eviction of thousands of forest dwellers.

LEGAL PROVISIONS UNDER FOREST RIGHT ACT

The Forest Rights Act has brought a metamorphosis in the Government perspective. It synthesized the antithesis of historical injustice done to the tribal's and forest dwellers during the post independence period. The Act constitutionally recognized individual and community rights over forest and legally empowered communities to protect and manage the forest.

The legal provisions under FRA, 2006, and FR Rules, 2007 and FR (Amendment) Rules, 2012 are presented below:

CFR Area, Protection and Management under FRA

It is very important to understand and know about the status of land in a village before filing a claim for IFR and CFR rights. Once we know the nature of land (status of forest land in and around our village), it would be easier for us to trace the extent of land to be claimed under IFR or in CFR. Since FRA is applied over the forest land, it is very important to know the Status of forest land/nature of land of the village. Thus based on the status of forest land available in and around a village, we can divide all the villages into three groups to trace and understand the scope of the CFR rights to be claimed and to be recognized under CFR:

1. **A Revenue village surrounded by revenue villages from its four sites:** Since we find hardly any disputes between/amongst revenue villages over the revenue village boundaries, now the scope of Community Forest Resource area would be limited to the available forest land area within the village boundary only. Before finalizing the total CFR area, we have to separate the forest area under individual occupation (of all STs and OTFDs) and the rest forest land would automatically come under the CFR area. Since all the RoR (Khata Nos and Plots Nos are available in these revenue villages, we hardly need use of GPS machine in these villages. Thus in these villages, the CFR area would be limited to the forest land available in the revenue village itself.
2. **A revenue village surrounded by reserve forest from its one to three sides:** In these villages, the scope of the CFR area would be definitely more than the 1st typology of villages. While the CFR area within the village can be traced out based on the method applied for the first type of village, the CFR area outside the revenue village boundary (of the reserve forest) can easily be found out using GPS machine or by measuring it in a plain table

method. Now the scope of the CFR area of these villages includes revenue forest land available within the village boundary plus reserve forest area available outside the revenue village boundary.

3. **A forest or un-surveyed village located inside the reserve forest area**: This type of village might be surrounded by revenue villages from its one to two sites. In these villages, since the village boundary is to be determined by the villagers afresh, the CFR area would come within the village boundary itself. In this village also we can find out the total CFR area leaving the IFR area. We can also use GPS machine or plain table method to measure the extent of land and the CFR area of these villages. Thus based on the above method/typology developed we can understand and trace the scope of the CFR area in different villages.

PROCESS OF FORMATION OF CFR PROTECTION AND MANAGEMENT COMMITTEE BY THE GRAM SABHA

In this context, two situations are likely to arise at the Gram Sabha level in the whole State over CFR Protection and Management:

1. Where formal CFR protection and Management is already going on; and
2. where CFR protection and Management is going on but not in a formal way.

In the first situation, the Gram Sabha has to reform the CFR P&M Committees in the line of FRA provisions and has to inform the SDLC for taking over the Forest Protection and Management of CFR by it as per FRA.

In the second situation, the Gram Sabha has to form a CFR P&M Committee in the line of FRA provisions and has to inform the SDLC of the taking over the Forest Protection and Management of CFR by it as per FRA. In both the cases, the

Gram Sabhas shall authorize the CFR P&M Committee to execute the decisions of the Gram Sabha and to protect, regenerate and manage the forest as per Section 3(1) (i) of the FRA, 2006.

As per Section 4(f) of the RF (Amendment) rules, 2012, the committee constituted under clause(e) shall prepare conservation and management plan for community forest resources. But it is strongly suggested that CFR P&M plan prepared by the committee should be approved by the Gram Sabha. While preparing the CFR P&M Plan, the CFR P&M Committee also can take the technical support from the Forest Department and Other Line Departments, Govt. of Odisha.

It is also suggested that Gram Sabha can also send its resolution ascertaining the formation of the CFR P&M Committee (and details of the members) to the SDLC for information.

The CFR P&M Committee shall act as the executive body of the Gram Sabha (the General Body). While the Gram Sabha would be the Permanent Body, the EC of the Gram Sabha would be elected by the Gram Sabha for a particular period of time and can be dissolved on the basis of resolution of Gram Sabha.

SALIENT FEATURES OF CFR PROTECTION AND MANAGEMENT PLAN

As per the National Working Plan Code, 2014 "community rights related to use of community forest resources like minor forest produce, grazing grounds, water bodies, etc. recognized under the provisions of the Forest Rights Act, 2006 can be exercised within the frame of sustainable management defined under section 2(o) of Biodiversity Act, 2002."

Further it stressed "details of existing rights are to be provided so as to assess their sustainability, reasoning for their continuity and enhancement of productivity. Therefore, special efforts in the form of good practice guidance, capacity building, orientation, provision of incentives for the exercise of rights would need to be provided to maintain the sustainability of these forests. This will also facilitate Gram Sabha to monitor the working of the committee constituted under clause 4 (e) of Forest Rights Rules 2012, which shall prepare a conservation and management plan for community forest resources in order to sustainably and equitably manage such community forest resources for the benefit of forest dwelling scheduled tribes and other traditional forest dwellers."

The National Working Plan Code 2014 suggests the following important aspects for the preparation of working plan:

- **Maintenance, Conservation and Enhancement of Biodiversity:** Forest composition and distribution, plant species diversity, status of biodiversity conservation of forests, status of species prone to over exploitation, conservation of genetic resources, fauna and their habitats, threats and challenges to wildlife, protection and management of fauna;
- **Maintenance and Enhancement of Forest Health and Vitality:** Status of regeneration, area affected by forest fires, area damaged by natural calamities, area protected from grazing, lopping practices, area infested by invasive weed species in forests, incidences of pest and diseases, forest degradation and its drivers;
- **Conservation and Maintenance of Soil and Water Resources:** Assessment of excess runoff from discharge zone and conservation measures for soil, groundwater, and soil moisture. Area treated under soil and water conservation measures, duration of water flow in the selected seasonal streams, wetlands in forest areas, water level in the wells in the vicinity (up to 5 km) of forest area, status of aquifers;
- **Maintenance and Enhancement of Forest Resource Productivity:** Growing stock of wood/bamboo, increment

in volume of identified timber species, efforts towards enhancement of forest productivity through quality plantation activities, carbon stock, carbon sequestration and mitigation;

- **Optimization of Forest Resource Utilization:** Recorded removal of timber, fuel wood, bamboo/rattans, and locally important NTFPs including MAPs, demand and supply of timber and important non-timber forest produce, removal of fodder, valuation of the products.

MAINTENANCE AND ENHANCEMENT OF SOCIAL, ECONOMIC, CULTURAL AND SPIRITUAL BENEFITS

Status of woman empowerment, labour welfare, use of indigenous knowledge, extent of cultural/sacred groves, social customs, status of compliance of Forest Right Act (FRA), other rights and concessions, ecotourism areas and activities, etc.

While the suggested aspect by the National Working Plan Code 2014 are important for the protection and management of CFR and its plan, it still emphasized on the Forest Department controlled forest protection and does not recognizes "CFR area" as a new typology of forest area recognized under FRA exclusively under the protect and management of the Gram Sabha.

Thus it is strongly suggested that each Gram Sabha shall be free to develop its own simple format for CFR protection, management and conservation plan which its members can better understand. The CFR protection and management plan should also comprise the existing rules and regulations governing forest, access, use, protection and conservation.

STATUS OF FOREST LAND AND FOREST ADMINISTRATION IN ODISHA

As per the notification by the Govt. of Odisha, the total geographical area of the State is 155707 Sq Km (38459629 acres). Out of the total district geographical area 60.94 percent is revenue land (other than revenue forest land) and rest 39.16 percent of the total area is forest land. It is reported that out of 39.16 percent of forest land, the State Forest Department has 43.32 percent of forest land including the reserved forest in the State while around 52.26 percent are Revenue forest land including the protected forest and rest 4.40 percent forest land is District Level Committee (DLC), DLC lands are those non-forest revenue land filed on affidavit by the State Government before the Supreme Court in connection with WP(c) No. 202/1995.

As per the state government norms, the forests of the State are protected and managed by the Forest Department. The mandate of the Forest Department is to protect forests and wildlife, ensure scientific management and enrich forest resource with active cooperation of the local communities.

To protect the forest, there are 7 Forest Circles and 37 Forest Divisions under the Principal Chief Conservator of Forests, 1 Circle and 12 Wildlife Divisions with territorial jurisdiction and Nandankanan under the Chief Wildlife Warden and Principal Chief Conservator of Forests (Wildlife). Besides, there are 2 National Parks, 18 Sanctuaries, 3 Circles and 19 Kendu leaf Divisions under Addl. Principal Chief Conservator of Forests (KL) engaged in collection and processing of Kendu leaves. There are 165 K.L. Ranges formed in the State for collection and processing of Kendu leaf. There are 8 working plan Divisions, one Forest Resources Survey Division, and two Silviculture Divisions looking into preparation of working plans, resource inventory and forest research respectively. There are 221 Forest Rangers, 60 Wildlife Ranges in the State for Protection & Management of Forest and Wildlife. In addition to regular staff, there are 19 APR units deployed in 19 Forest Divisions Odisha to assist the forest staff in protection activities. Further there are 364 Forest Protection Squads in the State.

Each squad comprises 10 local youths who are engaged in protection activities. There are 208 Forest Check Gates set up at vulnerable points all over the State to check transit of forest produce and to control forest and wild life offences. 590 VHF stations and 880 Walky-Talkies are operational in the State for strengthening communication network to be used for monitoring protection activities. Besides, there are 12,413 Vana Sarankshan Samitis (VSS) protecting a total of 11530 sq. km of forests and 501 Eco-Development Committees (EDC) have been formed so far in protected areas to look into the protection activities. There are 616 firearms made available to the field staff for their use during protection activities. Besides, State Forestry Awards are conferred, on the occasion of World Forestry Day, every year for outstanding work in afforestation and plantation activities to Gram Panchayats, Educational Institutions and students.

COMMUNITY FOREST PROTECTION AND MANAGEMENT IN ODISHA

Odisha is nationally and internationally recognized for its unique community based forest protection and management. This community based forest protection and management in the State has long history from 1980s when the forest were cut down in the method of coupe system by the forest department giving lease to the private contractors. The forests were totally ruined where community depended for their day to day sustenance. As a result, the community people of nearby villages got together and started protecting the roots which naturally regenerated into forest. In many districts, these forests have become dense forest. However, when the forest cover increased, the forest department by motivating the people in the name of environment and by offering financial support has brought them into the Joint Forest Management (JFM) fold and formed Vana Surakhyana Sammitte (VSS) at the village level.

In many cases, these villages do have community based forest protection and management practices, the forest Department still continue to enlist them in the list of JFMC formed in the State. However, there are certain community based forest protection groups in the State who rejected the offer of the forest department and denied becoming JFM. They continued to be called CFM having full control over the forest resources.

Now after the enactment of FRA, the Gram Sabha can reclaim these forests under B and C forms and establish Gram Sabha's full control over the forest. In many villages, the VSS area assigned under JFM are small area in comparison to the vast CFR area/traditional forest area of the Gram Sabha claimed as CFR. Now these VSS area automatically comes under the CFR area. Since FRA has the provision of a forest protection and management committee exclusively of the community people of a village (Gram Sabha) and has empowered the community people to protect and manage the forest by themselves, the relevance of VSS committee is no more in the village. Besides, while FRA has a constitutional mandate, VSS formed under JFM are based on executive orders having no legal backup.

STATUS OF FOREST LAND & CFR IN MAYURBHANJ DISTRICT OF ODISHA

Mayurbhanj district is coming under the Central Zone of Odisha. The total geographical area of the district is 10418 sq. km. (2573246 acres) and is the biggest district of Odisha. Out of the total district geographical areas, 56.92 percent is revenue land (other than revenue forest land) and only 43.08 percent of the total area is forest land. The forest area of the district is 1108600.22 acres which is 43.08 percent of the total geographical area of the district. Out of 1108600.22 acres total of forest land, 261768.13 acres constituting 23.61 per cent of the total forest areas is categorized as Revenue Forest Land while 823087.98 constituting 74.25 percent acres are under the State Forest Department and rest 23744.11 acres constituting percent are DLC land.

As per the FRA Implementation Status report produced by the SLMC till 31st Jan 2015, in total 708 Community Forest Rights (CFR) claims (354 in 'B' and 354 in 'C' form) have been filed at Gram Sabha out of which only 180 CFR claims (90 in 'B' form and 90 in 'C' form filed (185 in B form and 8 in C form) have been settled and till date and only 88 CFR titles (44 filed in 'B' & 44 in 'C' form) have been distributed over 38836.74 (19418.37 against B and 19418.37 against C). However there is problem in the data since both the area claimed under 'B' and 'C' are same. Rest of the claims are shown pending in the status report of SLMC.

VILLAGE LEVEL CFR PROTECTION & MANAGEMENT: A CASE IN ODISHA

The Revenue village Duvia comes under Budhikhamari Gram Panchayat of Baripada Block of Mayurbhanj district. This village is inhabited at a distance of 15 km from the block and district headquarters. The village Duvia is surrounded by Budhikhamari Reserve Forest in the East and South, Revenue village Jagannathpur in the West, Revenue village Aahari in the North. There are two hamlets in the village Duvia, i.e. Duvia-A and Duvia-B. As per 2011 Census Report, there are 110 households in the revenue village Duvia. The total population of the village is 535 (261 male and 274 female). This village is inhabited mostly by Kolha tribe which constitutes 90 percent of the total population followed by 8 percent and the population of tribal is 519 (257 male and 262 female). Rest 2 percent of the populations are OBC (Mahanta) community. Census 2011 also records 209 (134 male and 75) literate people in the village.

STATUS OF LAND

From the RoR information of the village, the last survey and settlement in the village was done in 1970s. The revenue village Duvia comes under Budhikhamari RI Circle and Betanati Thana (No.9). As per the RoR information, there are total 102 khatas in the village. Out of which only 3 khata (khata No. 82, 83 and 84 having total 150 plots having 40.98 acres are government lands and rest 99 khata belongs to the private land holders having 559 plots and 286. 09 acres in the village. One khata No. 81/17 having plot no.284 and 135 acres belong to the Secretary of Nanak School, Duvia. Thus the total area of the revenue village Duvia is 286.09+40.98=327.07 acres only. Out of the total government land, forest land is 19.82 acres constituting 48.36 percent. Besides, around 561.42 acres of Budhikhamari RF the CFR area is surrounded by the village from East and South which the community people have been protecting since last 1970s.

STATUS OF LIVELIHOODS

As per the RoR of the village Duvia, most of the families are legally landless. Most of the families depend upon agriculture and NTFP collection from the forest. In addition to agriculture, goatery and labour work are the main source of the livelihoods in the village. Most of the families in the village make Sabai daudi (rope) in the village.

STATUS OF CFR CLAIM AND COMMUNITY FOREST RESOURCES

The Community rights claim in B form and C form for community rights over community resources have been filed by the Duvia Gram Sabha at the SDLC on dated 17th Nov 2014. Before submission of the CFR claims, field verification of the CFR area was done on 24th August 2014 in the presence of the SDLC representatives. The traditional CFR boundary/forest boundary have been verified/mapped by GPS machine and CFR map have been generated with the help of the SDLC and worker of with help of Vasundhara (State based organization working on FRA). Besides, a series of Gram Sabha meetings were held in the Duvia including the Gram Sabha on 23 July 2014.

STATUS OF FOREST SPECIES

Trees: The CFR of the Duvia Gram Sabha is dominated by natural-Sal tree, followed by Asan, Charkoli, Kendu, Harida, Bahada, Dha tree, Putuda, Mahula, Atundi, Kochila, Jhodi, Pia Sala, Rai fruits, Jamu, Sunari, Rohini, Jalhai, Gondsadua, Sisu, Gambhari, Mudmudika, Kuluchi, Khakada, Masundi,Neema, Karanja, Kaliruka,etc. Plantation of Akasi, Ukalipotash and Teak have been done by the Forest Department in the year 1987-88 and 1995-96 in the village.

Creepers: The main creepers available in the CFR area of Duvia are Suam, Satabari, Ramdantuni, Bhui Kokharu, Pitalu, Banyaalu, Panpatra Alu, Panialata, Tunga alu, Talmudi, Bhilimba, Sialipatra found very less in the CFR area etc.

Animals: Animal which live in the CFR area of Duvia area are Rabbits, Siala, Fox, Jackle, Katasa, Bana bilei, Hetabagh (goat), monkey (Pati Mankada) etc.

Migratory Animals: which comes to the CFR area of the Duvia in different seasons are Elephant, Pachakhia, Baraha, Wolf, Mayur and barking Deer.

Birds: The important birds in the CFR area are Parrot-(middle), Kapata, Koili, Boni, Harada Chadei, Haladi Basanta, Gundari, Kitari, Bana Kukuda, Kumbhatua, Owls, Rati Chora, Tiki Chadhei, Bai Chadei, Ghara Chatia (house sparrow), Para (rock peogeon), (Indian baya), Bani (Indian common myna), Jungle Bani (Indian jungle myna), Pecha (spotted owlet), Sua (rose ringed parakit), Bada Sua (large alexandrine parakit).

Fauna: The important reptiles found in the CFR area of the village Duvia are Enduo (*Calotes versicolar*), Tampa (*Naja naja kunthia*), Naga (*Naja naja naja*), Dhamna (*Ptyas mucosus*), Pani dhanda (*Xenocropis*), Rana (*Bungarus fasciatus*), Chiti (*Bungarus caeruleus*), Ajagara (*Python molurus*), Matibiradi (*Amphiesma stolata*) Godhi (*Varanus benghalensis*), Ahiraja (*Opheophagus hanahor),* King cobra Sqaurrel-Dalua Musha, Gadhi, Neula.

Fuel woods: The main fuel used in the village are dry leaves, dry branches, dry stumps and dry tree. The trees mostly used for fuel wood are Kulchi, Gandhsalua, and Khaka.

Use of Timber and Poles: Timbers used for home construction in the villages are Sal, Palasi, Kuruma, Gandhasalua, Jalhi, dha, Palasi, Asana.

Fencing: For fencing they used the plants, called "Ajatia Jhota" meanse non-timber plants are Porasi, Uruchi, Khokada, Gandhasalua, Aatundi, Kalarukha etc.

Commercial items of NTFP collected from the CFR area are Sal leaf, Jhuna (*Shorea robusta*), Tola (*Madhuca indica*), Mahula (*Madhuca indica*), Kendu (*Diospyros melanoxylon*), Mushrooms, Danta kathi (*Shorea robusta*) Sal leaves, Char seeds, Sal fruit, tooth brushes and Mushrooms.

FOREST FRUITS PLANTS

The important fruits plan available in the Duvia CFR area are Kendu (*Diospyros melanoxylon*), Jamukoli (*Syzygium cumini*), Tolafala (*Madhuca indica*), Barakoli (*Ziziphus mauritiana*), Bela (*Aegle marmelos*), Harida (*Terminalia chebula*), Bahada (*Terminalia bellerica*), etc.

LEAFY VEGETABLES/SAG

The important forest leafy vegetables found and collected from CFR area area Mati saga, gachha saga, bhuin chhati ,

Thalkudi (*Centella asiatica*), Bhadalia (*Olax Scandens*), Barada (*Bauhinia purpurea*), Odonga (*Cycas circinalis*), Muthi Saga (*Polegonum plebium*), Kalama Saga (*Ipomea*), Pita Saga (*Molugo pentaphylla*), Chakunda (*Cassia tora*), Poisaga, Limba saga (*Azadiracta indica*), Khada Saga (*Amaranthus sps*), poisaga.

Mushrooms

There are different types of wild mushrooms collected from the CFR area of Duvia Gram Sabha i.e. (rootka chhatu), Kunda chhatu, Bali chhatu, Nada Chhatu, Hunka and Mhal chhatu, Bausha chhatu, Badabali chhatu and Manda chhatu etc.

Tubers

The important tubers collected from the Duvia CFR area are Tunga, Karaba, Pichhuli, Suta alu, Kasa alu, Kanta alu, Pita Alu etc. are climbers.

Sabai Grass

It is generally grown in the private land. This grass is used for rope making and every family in the village is engaged in cultivation and rope making out of this Sabai grass. There is much scope to start entrepreneurship on sabai grass in the village and even in the nearby villages.

FOREST SPECIES USED IN CULTURAL ACTIVITIES

Palasa (*Butesmonosperma*), Satabari (*Asparagus recemosus*), Bhalia (*Semicarpus anacardium*), Bana malati (*Aganosma*), Amla (*Phyllanthus emblica*), Odanga (*Cycas circinalis*), Aswasta (*Cycas circinalis*), Aswasta (*Ficus*), Sahada (*Streblus asper*), Jamu (*Syzizium cumini*), Bara (*Ficus benghalensis*), Neem (*Azadirachta indica*), bela (*Aegle marmelous*), Harida (*Terminalia chebula*) siali (*Bauhinia vahlii*), Gohira, Ashoka (*Saroka asoka*), Tola, Mahula etc.

MAJOR THREATS TO THE FOREST

The major threats identified for the CFR area are:

1. Forest fires which generally happened from the month of Feb to June in every year.
2. Natural calamities, during cyclone many trees from the forest are uprooted.
3. Illegal tree felling is not totally avoided. Many neighbouring villagers are still engaged in stealing trees from CFR area.
4. Unregulated grazing has been a major threat for the growth of forest which needs to be regulated.
5. Despite forest protection rules, due to ignorance at the community level many wild animals and birds i.e. Squarrel, Rabbit, birds (Kapata) Baga, Godhi, Kaincha, Musha (Gatua, Dalua, Chuti Musha, Chati (Ant)-Kurkuti-(Kai) etc are being hunted.

DUTIES AND RESPONSIBILITIES OF GRAM SABHA TOWARDS FOREST PROTECTION

1. All the members of the Duvia Gram Sabha have the duties towards forest and wildlife as per the provisions under Section 5 of the Forest Rights Act, 2006.
2. All the members of the Duvia Gram Sabha individually and collectively ensure protection of the forests against fire, grazing, illegal felling, theft of forest produce, poaching of wildlife and encroachment of the community forest land. They also ensure protection of wildlife.
3. All the member families of the Gram Sabha have to contribute for the CFR protection and management.
4. All the members of the Duvia Gram Sabha obey the rules and regulations devised by the Gram Sabha for the protection and management of CFR area and other such rules framed.

5. It shall be the duty of all members of the Gram Sabha to prevent forest and wild life offence and pass on relevant information in this regard to the Executive members (CFR P&MC) of the Gram Sabha.
6. The Gram Sabha members shall participate in preparing long term and short term forest protection plan for integrated development of the village(s) and for the conservation, development and sustainable management of the CFR.
7. The members of the Gram Sabha have the powers to elect, remove any elected member of the CFR P&MC including the President, Vice-President/Secretary. Additional Secretary/Treasurer etc by a simple majority of the members present and voting if in eye of the Gram Sabha is satisfied that the concerned member does not discharge his/her duties satisfactorily. All these process take place in the Gram Sabha meeting.
8. The Gram Sabha can forward any forest offenders to the police for necessary legal action.
9. The Gram Sabha can ask any Line Department of Government of Odisha for capacity building of members of CFR P&MC and other members of the Gram Sabha on different aspects i.e. forest protection and management, planning, silviculture, nursery technology, forest laws, accounting and book keeping etc.
10. The Gram Sabha shall ensure proper participation of women and other weaker sections in decision making process of the Gram Sabha and CFR P&MC.
11. The Gram Sabha selects Forest Advisory Committee to guide CFR P&MC in due discharge of their duties and in resolving disputes.
12. The Gram Sabha shall authorize the CFR P&MC to issue "Transit Pass" for the transportation of MFP and Timber collected in and out of the CFR area.

13. All the members of Gram Sabha protect the forest from fire.

MANAGEMENT AND AUDIT OF FOREST FUND BY GRAM SABHA

1. There is a Gram Sabha Forest Account for depositing the money collected from different sources by the Gram Sabha.
2. The CFR P&MC is responsible for the management of Forest fund of the Gram Sabha and other resources received from any Government Departments, fund internally generated, if any. For this purpose, a joint account called Gram Sabha Forest Account has been opened in 2013-14. The joint Bank account is in the name of the President, Secretary and Treasurer of the CFR P&MC. Presently Rs. 2,30,000 is deposited in the account.
3. Any withdrawal from the Gram Sabha Forest Account can be done only prior approval of the Gram Sabha in this regard and a copy of the said resolution shall be endorsed by the President of CFR P&MC.
4. The funds deposited into the Gram Sabha Forest Account are utilized towards the conservation and development of forest, development of the village. The Secretary and Treasurer are responsible for the submission of the Monthly account and maintenance of the Cash Book of the Gram Sabha Forest Account.
5. An independent body from the Gram Sabha members is annually appointed by the Gram Sabha who do annual audit of income and expenditure incurred by the CFR P&MC and presents it in the GB meeting of the Gram Sabha. Besides, the CFR P&MC submits the utilization Certificate relating to the expenditure in the Gram Sabha meeting. In case, if the supports/expenditures incurred are from the line departments of the Govt. of Odisha, the

concerned line department can do audit with the approval of then Gram Sabha.

REFERENCES

Asher, M. and N. Agarwal (2005), Recognising the Historical Injustice: Campaign for Forest Rights Act, Pune: National Centre for Advocacy Studies.

Bijoy, C.R. and K. Raman (2003), The Real Story: Adivasi Movement to Recover Land, Economic and Political Weekly 38(20): 17-23.

Bindra, P. (2005), UPA's Tribal Bill: Tigers' Death Warrant, The Pioneer, 23 April.

Chaterjee, P. (2004), The Politics of the Governed: Reflections on Popular Politics in Most of the World. New York: Columbia University Press.

Diani, M. (1995), Green Networks: A Structural Analysis of the Italian Environmental Movement, Edinburgh: Edinburgh University Press.

Dutta, R. and B. Yadav (2005), Supreme Court on Forest Conservation. Delhi: Universal Law Publishing Co.

FRA Status Report (SLMC, Odisha), 2015.

Ganapathy, N. (2005), Environment Ministry Strikes at the Root of the Tribal Rights Bill, The Indian Express, 13 April.

Ghosh, S. (2007), Commons Lost and "Gained"? Forest Tenures in the Jungle Mahals of South West Bengal. Working Paper No. 7. Norwich: Overseas Development Group, University of East Anglia.

GOI (1986), Report of the Study Group on Land Holding Systems in Tribal Areas. New Delhi: Planning Commission of India, 1986.

GOI (2005), Joining the Dots: The Report of the Tiger Task Force. New Delhi: Government of India, Union Ministry of Environment and Forests.

GOI (2010), Report of the National Committee on Forest Rights. New Delhi, Ministry of Environment and Forests,

Gopalakrishnan, S. (2005), Missing the Woods for Trees, Combat Law 4(2).

Gopalakrishnan, Shankar (June-July 2005), Missing the Woods for the Trees. Combat Law 4(4).

Guha, R. (1989), The Unquiet Woods: Ecological Change and Peasant Resistance in the Himalaya. Berkeley, CA: University of California Press.

Government Bhulekh Report.

Kapur, Mehta, A. and A. Shah (2003), Chronic Poverty in India: Incidence, Causes and Policies, World Development 31(3): 491-511.

Kaur, N. (2002), Targeting Tribal People: The Union Ministry of Environment and Forests seeks to clear 12.5 lakh hectares of Forest Land by evicting its 10 million strong tribal population, Frontline.

Kumar, K., P.R. Choudhary, S. Sarangi, P. Mishra and S. Behera (2005), A Socio-Economic and Legal Study of Scheduled Tribes' Land in Orissa. Unpublished study commissioned by the World Bank, Washington DC.

MoEF (2010), Decision on Grant of Forest Clearance in Kalahandi and Rayagada districts of Orissa for the proposal submitted by the Orissa Mining Corporation for Bauxite Mining in Lanjigarh Bauxite Mines.

Pathak, A. (1994), Contested Domains: The State, Peasants and Forests in Contemporary India. New Delhi: Sage Publications.

Prabhu, P. (2005), The Right to Live with Dignity, Seminar 552: 14.

Prasad, Archana (30 December 2006). Survival at Stake. Frontline 23 (26).

Sarin, M. (2003), Forest Conservation is too complex an issue to be resolved by Executive Fiat, Down to Earth 15 July. http://www.downtoearth.org.in/node/13145 (accessed 10 January 2012).

Sinha, A. (2008), Crores Lost in Timber Protests: Yet to Shut Down, The Telegraph, 14 May.

Shah, A. and B. Guru (2005), Poverty in Remote Rural Areas in India: A Review of Evidence and Issues. CPRC-IIPA Working Paper No. 21. New Delhi: Indian Institute of Public Administration.

6

Green Business and Sustainable Economic Development

INTRODUCTION

Green business is an environment friendly business practice. These practices might include the use of organic and natural products to build its facilities, tighter protections against emissions, environmentally responsible sourcing of supplies and designing organizations and processes in order to achieve efficient and economical use of resources. Green business is to adopt principles, policies and practices that improve the quality of life for customers and protect resources. Using renewable energy resources, enhancing material recyclability, reducing toxic dispersion are all eco-efficient practices while doing green business. Management of green business can be considered from the cost point of view and may be an opportunity for saving. The perception of "green business" emerged at the end of the 20th century in the wake of the ever-increasing public concern about the sustainability of economic development. Later on with the growing awareness, some environmental issues such as the accelerating depletion of natural resources and the deterioration of environmental quality have emerged in the economy. Sustainable development is one of the pillars of strategic management. Especially, economical and equitable use of resources has been one of the most fashionable approaches. Companies started to give more attention to environmental concerns for securing future existence of their resources and business.

According to Hawken (1995) now a business venture has been facing three types of issues. These are what it will take, what it will make and what it wastes. What it takes is materials from the environment, (its ecosystem) through extracting, mining, cutting, hunting and other means. What it makes is the products of commerce, goods and services that derived from the natural environment through the process of conversion and transformation. What it wastes represents eco-costs arising from garbage, pollution and destruction of natural systems, which are the consequences of taking and making processes. However, these costs are not internalized in most of the accounting systems so far.

The critical importance of industrial greening is highlighted by a consideration of the factors that contribute to large-scale environmental deterioration. Environmental Impact equals a product of population (P), times affluence (A), times technology (T) (Ehrlich & Ehrlich, 1991).

Mathematically, **I = P x A x T**; where, P and A are socio-political phenomena and are beyond the control of an industry or business. However, the technology co-efficient is controllable. Technology applications reflect consumption of resources in qualitative and quantitative terms, energy used and the efficiency level of production and marketing and disposal of wastes. These are controllable technology decisions that can increase or reduce eco-costs. The goal is to reduce the use of unsustainable technologies and increase the use of clean technologies to reduce in the long run T to zero which theoretically means I (Environmental Impact) would be zero at any quantity of P and A.

Greening product or market is viewed as the outcome of rational strategic choice. It may thus involve the search for different types of competitive advantage (Gladwin & Eidlin, 1992). Because of staggering pollution levels and the diversity of environmental concerns, a wide range of pressures is coming to bear upon industry/firms from many sides. The intensity of these pressures varies by country, sector, industry and firm. It is clear, however, that firms need to respond in order to ensure further use of scarce resources, public and political legitimacy, profitability and financial assurance (Fischer & Schot, 1993).

In the developed countries, the surge of environmental consciousness that followed Earth Day in 1990 washed over the market place rapidly. Poll after poll, consumers claimed they were willing to change their buying habits and even pay more for products to protect the environment (Pearce, 1990; Codington, 1993; Davis, 1992; Ottaman, 1993). Manufacturers got the messages, reports that the percentage of new packaged products making some kind of green claim more than doubled between 1989 and 1990, rising from 4.5 percent to 11.4 percent of the total.

The objectives of this chapter are to analyse the basic concepts of green business, its different components, and the factors influencing green business, the business greening agents and green growing groups. Secondly, the paper throws light on the government initiatives to promote this concept to maintain ecological balance, safety environment for attaining sustainable development in the state. Thirdly, some appropriate steps may be suggested for the state to gain competitive advantage by following the philosophy of green marketing and practicing the green business strategies.

The methodologies adopted in this chapter were in the line of collection of data and analyzing them to reach its desired objectives. Here the data were collected from the secondary sources and then by reviewing some literatures and some specific researches, the outcomes have been reflected.

In addition to this, several focus group discussions were conducted among the development practitioners and environmentalists on the topic to enrich the paper.

GREEN BUSINESS AND SUSTAINABLE ECONOMIC DEVELOPMENT

Green business is an attempt to characterize a product as being environment friendly. It holds the view that marketing, which is a part of business, not only has to satisfy customers in particular, but also has to take into account the interests of the society in general. All those who are affected by the activities of a business should be kept in mind while setting the objectives and the policies of an organization. This has already helped increasing the recent trend towards the "greening" of the companies. Sustainable consumption and sustainable development are the by-product of two sustainable economic development. Sustainable development refers to maintaining long-term economic, social and environmental capital, while sustainable consumption becomes the way of life. Sustainable consumption is using resources in a way that minimizes harm to the environment while supporting the well-being of people. Realizing the importance of people's concern for a healthy environment to live and preferring environmental friendly products and services to consume, marketers these days are trying to capitalize on the same to ensure sustainable growth and using these concepts in designing their strategies.

Sustainable development is a development processes that carter to the needs of the present without jeopardizing the needs of future generations. In this context, the focus should be on the establishment as well as management of enterprises with minimal negative impact on the global or local environment, community, society, or economy. The area of concern must include energy, water sustainability, resource management, transportation, healthy work environment, communications, sustainable public procurement, sustainable consumption and production.

One of the prime business strategies for sustainable growth has taken the shape of Green Marketing. Green Marketing can be viewed both as a type of marketing and marketing philosophy. As a type of marketing, it is like industrial or service marketing, and is concerned with marketing of green products and to position them as green brands. Green marketing runs parallel to the societal marketing concept and espouses the view that satisfying customers is not enough and marketers should take into account ecological interests of the society as a whole. It is a part of Corporate Social Responsibility (CSR). The strategy for green marketing can help to get more customers and make more money. Marketers should analyze the changing consumer attitudes while recognizing the role of the companies can play in protecting the environment to ensuring the well being of the society. They must realize that green marketing is not purely altruistic – it can be a profitable endeavor for sustainable growth.

GREENING OF BUSINESS

Furthermore, green business practices are still far from being universally accepted and applied by business entities around the world, with perceptible differences of business penetration by the "green" ideas in various countries. This is on account of many reasons, that the "greening of business" is still largely perceived as an extra burden by increase in cost or incurring loss in revenue, and the other reason being related to the national specific in terms of cultural, political, and economic differences. Green business is an organization that is committed to the principles of environmental sustainability in its operations. It strives to use renewable resources, and tries to minimize the negative environmental impact of its activities. In this perception, "greening" of business is part of a long-term strategy of becoming sustainable, i.e. being able to achieve business tasks in the way that does not develop any threat – economic, social or environmental – for both current and future generations.

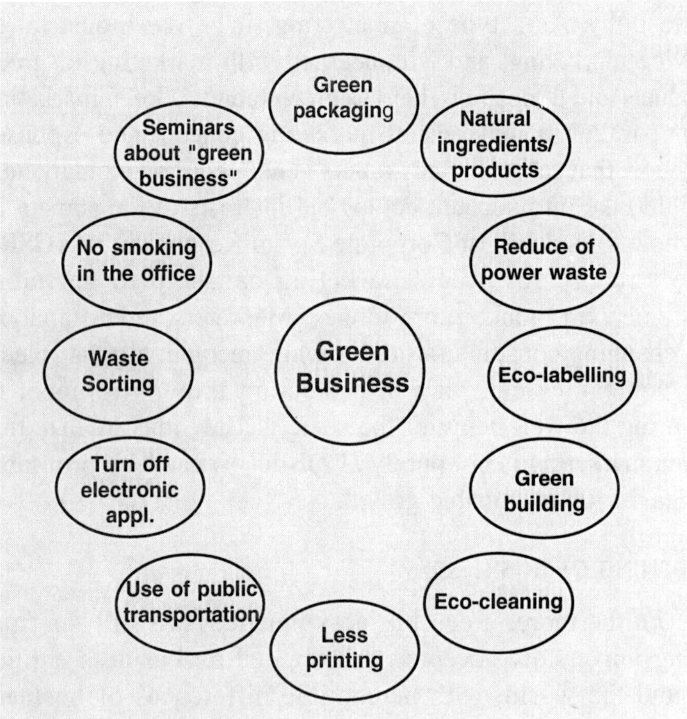

BUSINESS GREENING AGENTS

The shifting of mindset from general business to the business with green trend can be attributed exclusively to the initiatives of business itself. One can distinguish three main agents of the process: consumers, governments, and business, each of them in its own way contributing to the formation of "green request" to business in its own way.

Green consumer: A green consumer can be defined as an individual who purchases ecologically produced or eco-friendly products i.e. those are made, imported and traded without causing pollution, can be reused or utilized and evade the environmentally harmful consumption by saving water and energy, recycling and so on. Environmentally aware consumers can behave either individually or collectively. The individual green behaviour is clearly visible itself in personal decisions whether to act in a green way (e.g., recycle) and to pay more for a green product, or not. Collective action is taken through associations non-governmental associations (NGOs) which in turn contribute to foster the environmental awareness of the public. Furthermore, by rising concerns about the harmful effects of particular industrial activities and promoting environmentally safe practices, NGOs exert a social pressure on business and government.

Government: Recognizing the impact of human actions on the environment and acting under pressure from consumers (voters) and various NGOs, governments (local, national or supranational) provide a regulatory framework for business operations, with an aim to restrict the environmentally harmful and to regulate the environmentally friendly business behavior with promptitude.

Go green business: It is a multifaceted process; there are various practices that can be applied when business wants to shift to a green behaviour. Broadly speaking, an environmentally aware business should participate at least in one of "4 Rs" – reduction, reuse, recycling, and recovery (Kassaye, 2001*)*.Each of those "Rs" can be achieved through several practices, some of which might serve the purpose of more than one "R".

ACTIVE PARTNERS FOR GREEN BUSINESS

These following groups are the active partners in real sense which poses challenges to industries or organizations:

Consumers: Consumers are increasingly better informed and becoming aware of the environmental impact of consumer products and are thus demanding that industry improves the environmental performance of its products. Today consumers are more enlightened and especially in developed countries, they even seek for sustainable development for their children.

Government: The threat of enforceable legislation and the rising costs of complying with environmental regulations and penalties in case of non-compliance are possible motivating factors for firms to incorporate environmental concerns in their strategies (Banerjee, 1998). In India, the Government enacted laws concerning pollution control and environmental protection, including Environment (Protection) Act 1986, the Air (Prevention & Control of Pollution) Act 1981 and the Water (Prevention & Control of Pollution) Act 1974. While environmental legislation represents the main pressure, increasing costs associated with managing emissions are also an important factor.

Investor: Investors are increasingly examining the environmental records of potential investments, and some are showing a tendency to invest in "Greener" companies. This behaviour is based on the expectations that these companies will benefit commercially from their green image and there are efficiency gains associated with the adoption of cleaner technologies (Beckenbach & Kahlenborn, 2016).

Community: Local communities represent a powerful pressure for improved environmental performance, particularly where firms are located in close proximity to residential areas. This is applicable to both developed and developing countries. Where problems and nuisance are associated with noise, vibration, and dirty/foul smell; local communities, both directly and indirectly through complaints to local environmental health departments are capable of bringing considerable pressure to reduce environmental problems. The result of many national polls tracking environmental concern among the general public indicate that environmental protection remains high on the agenda of the public in many countries, despite escalating economic woes in some areas. A negative public image can influence firms in this industry to adopt corporate environmentalism as a strategy to survive and grow in the market place. All the chemical corporations publicly affirm their commitment to environmental protection and have developed environmental mission statements or policy statements.

Business-to-business customers: They evaluate supplies on ISO 14000 standards, the environmental counterpart to ISO 9000, the International quality standard. Moreover, the buyer looks for suppliers who follow environmental friendly processes or Good Manufacturing Practices (GMP).

Employees: The interests and aspiration of the work force of trade unions represent potential pressure resulting in a strong interest in the environmental performance and health and safety aspects of the plant. Other stakeholders include environmentalist, academicians, scientific community, media, retailers, local government, suppliers and buyers. On the basis of the attitude and behaviour of all the corporate stakeholders, it is realized that however, the task of practicing green philosophy is quite challenging and full of pressures and tensions, but at the same time it offers enormous opportunities to corporate in today's highly competitive global environment.

TRENDS OF ECONOMIC DEVELOPMENT IN ODISHA

Government of India in general as well as State government of Odisha in particular are encouraging the green business concept through the implementation of various developmental schemes in different sectors like Primary, Secondary and Tertiary sectors. Here both the categories of governments try to achieve the goals of SDGs. Government of Odisha try to implement the essence of green business through the line departments, sectoral departments and through different plans, programme and institutions of Panchayati Raj and Drinking Water department. The themes of analysis are well explained in the following manner.

Actions at the national level are reflected at state and local levels, as governments revise building codes, leading the construction industry to source greener building materials. In Odisha, the concept of green business is being applied in sectors beyond manufacturing and retail, including agriculture, where growth continues apace in demand for organic products and food sources from growers who are paid a fair wage and use sustainable farming techniques. Business recognize their capacity to help solving/addressing global environmental and social challenges, and the most innate understanding the business case to addressing such issues as climate change, water scarcity, pollution, poverty, hunger, and inequality. Along with the initiatives by the non-government sectors, government sector has been trying to uphold the essence of sustainable development keeping the attributes of green business implementing different types of livelihood programmes through Mahatma Gandhi NREGA, NRLM, Skill Development Programme and the like. Odisha's economy passed through a transformation from "a growing economy" to "an economy at take-off stage". Growth rate picks up momentum with industries. Services sectors are drivers of growth. Pace of industrialization has been accelerated with the advantage of rich natural resources and available physical and human capital in the State. Continuous improvement in "ease of doing business" has further stimulated the process. Infrastructure development has been laudable, but the imperative need for its further up gradation is still high and pressing. Social and financial inclusion show signs of improvement, but are not complete. Human development indicators have improved. Odisha's economy continues on a path of steady improvement in its growth. In 2017-18, Odisha's GSDP is estimated to grow at 7.14 percent as against the national average of 6.5 percent for India. This follows a striking expansion of 10.39 percent in 2016-17. Over the past few years, the State is exhibiting strong catch-up growth, which is helping in the transformation of the economy.

The credit for the improvement in the growth rate of the State over the last five years must go to several development initiatives and far-sighted macro management of economy through the government initiatives. In the primary sectors i.e. agriculture and allied sectors, Government of Odisha tries to incorporate the concept of green business by implementing the organic farming, implement the System of Rice Intensification (SRI), use of organic fertilizers, vermi-compost, Jivamrut and the like. For marketing of these products, Government of Odisha has been doing it through ORMAS, a marketing society under the aegis of Government of Odisha and the producers are getting their actual product prices. Similarly, in case of the dairy farming, OMFED is doing the marvelous work in promoting the green business in the field of dairy farming in Odisha. In this connection, some sectors may be analyzed as follows.

AGRICULTURE

The year 2016-17 saw an unprecedented growth of nearly 20 percent in agriculture after a severe contraction of over (-) 13 percent in 2015-16. This was largely on account of vagaries of weather, and also the low base. Indeed that has been the story of the agriculture sector in the State. Although there has been a significant negative growth in every alternative year in the recent past, the annual average growth rate (CAGR) for the sector is 2.8 percent for the period 2011-17.

The State Government has launched a number of short gestation projects like Mega Lift Irrigation Projects, Deep Bore Well Construction Programme and Check Dam Construction Programme with a view to rapidly meet the irrigation needs of the farmers. The target is to bring an additional 10 lakh hectare of cultivable land under irrigation cover by the end of 2019. The schemes such as Accelerated Irrigation Benefit Programme (AIBP), Rural Infrastructure Development Fund (RIDF), JBIC, Rastriya Sam Vikas Yojna (RSVY), National Rural Employment Guarantee Scheme (NREGS), Western Odisha Development Council (WODC) and FFW are being implemented to achieve the desired objective, either directly or by way of convergence with other programmes. As of March 2017, 93 blocks out of the targeted 198 blocks have been covered under this initiative.

The State government has been taking strategic policy initiatives and making budgetary provisions for agriculture sector to address inherent constraints associated with over-dependence on rain-fed farming, inadequate irrigation coverage, low level of capital formation, over-dependence on paddy cultivation, slow pace of modernization, small land holdings, continued prevalence of old tenancy practices in some areas and above all frequent occurrence and impact of natural calamities on the performance of the sector. Many of these measures need to be re-assessed and perhaps further intensified to attain the desired results.

INDUSTRY

Industry sector has a unique importance for Odisha's economy. The share of the sector in Gross State Domestic

Product (GSDP) at 35 percent is significant and the manufacturing Gross Value Added (GVA) in the organized industrial sector is percent, which is much more than the corresponding national average. During 2016-17, the mining sector growth at 10 percent was robust while manufacturing and construction sectors grew at 5 and 6 percent, respectively.

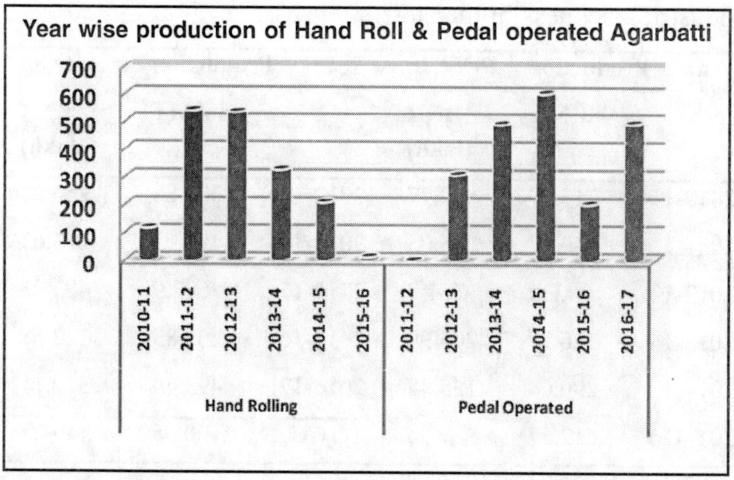

During 2017-18, the mining, manufacturing and construction sectors have estimated to grow moderately at 4.6 percent, while electricity, water supply and other utility services sub-sector is expected to clock a growth rate of percent. Over the past five years, the average growth (CAGR) for the industry sector as a whole has been 5.72 percent per annum. A disconcerting issue relates to the declining share of the industry in the GSDP is that it has declined from 43.6 percent in 2011-12 to an estimated 34.8 percent in 2017-18, even as the mineral-rich State has a huge potential for industrialization.

Industrialization process in Odisha led to setting up of 252 large and medium scale industries in 22 districts with a total investment of 92,788 crore rupees and employment of 1.18 lakh persons as of March 2017. Availability of mineral resources, particularly iron ore, bauxite and coal, and availability of water and power, and above all investor friendly policy of the State Government, has made Odisha a favoured destination for investors. Odisha is the leading State in the country in aluminum, both in terms of production and reserve capacity The State Government envisions a massive expansion of MSMEs in Odisha in the near future, while addressing the problem of industrial sickness in the state.

Year	**Production in MT**	**Price in INR (lakh)**	**Year**	**Production in MT**	**Price in INR (lakh)**
2010-11	116.29	69.77	2012-13	308.88	216.21
2011-12	540.37	335.03	2013-14	490.95	343.67
2012-13	535	331.7	2014-15	602.9	422.03
2013-14	326.97	205.99	2015-16	203.83	142.68
2014-15	290.04	125.42	2016-17	493.49	370.11
2015-16	12.57	7.54	TOTAL	2100.05	1494.7
TOTAL	1821.24	1075.45			

Production for the FY 2016-17 till March 2017

Through the state government initiatives, the production of Agarabati has been taken in the green business mode. The details are presented in the above table and graph.

To address the significant regional disparities in Odisha, the State Government has been implementing a number of development programmes with Central and State funding and has launched a number of specific initiatives. Out of these, important ones are Revised Long Term Action Plan (RLTAP), Biju KBK Plan, Biju Kandhamal O Gajpati Yojana, Gopabandhu Gramin Yojana (GGY), Western Odisha Development Council (WODC) and Special Development

Council. With the support of Government of India, the State government implemented Integrated Action Plan (IAP) in 18 tribal and backward districts of Odisha. These development initiatives have contributed in improving the development momentum in the backward regions of the State.

MACRO SECTORAL ECONOMIC GROWTH IN ODISHA

Agriculture and allied sectors cover the following economic activities:

(a) Crop production,

(b) Livestock,

(c) Forestry and logging, and

(d) Fishing.

The annual growth rates of this sector fluctuated significantly during 2011-12 to 2017-18. During 2016-17, the growth rate increased significantly to 19.65 percent on a low base due to higher production of crops. But it declined to negative growth of 4.70 percent in 2017-18 following lower crop production as per second advance estimate of crop statistics. During 2011-17, the Compound Annual Growth Rate (CAGR) was 2.8 percent only. Although contribution of agriculture and allied sector is moving downward from 62 percent in the 1950's to 19.98 percent in 2017, this sector still continues to be the main employment provider to small and marginal workers. Growth of this sector is important not only for ensuring food security and reduction of poverty in rural areas, but also to sustain growth of the rest of the economy.

The driver of growth of agriculture and allied sector can be identified as crop production with 13 percent share on an average in the total Gross State Value Added (GSVA). The shares of livestock, forestry and fishery sectors were estimated to be 3.00 percent, 2.36 percent and 2.08 percent respectively in 2017-18. The production of crops, which faces risks and uncertainties of natural calamities like deficient rainfall, pests attack, non-availability of credit, price fluctuations, failure of farming method, plays the dominant role in the growth of agriculture sector. As the cropping pattern of the State is cereal-centric, it requires more irrigation, more use of fertilizers, manures etc. More than 50 percent of the gross cropped areas are covered under cereal crops. Almost one third of the net area sown is irrigated, while two thirds remain unirrigated. Therefore, cultivation of other crops like pulses requiring less water need to be encouraged widely in un-irrigated areas to increase the level of production.

CONCLUSION

In retrospect, the green business will definitely promote the business enterprise along with the protection of health, sanitation and environment as well, which in turn will act as a catalytic agent for sustainable development. Therefore, in order to ensure this, some important points should be taken into account.

The concept of green brand through green business should be effectively communicated or marketed among the potential consumers. With increase in consumer awareness about green revolution, green products, green advertising and people's changing attitude from non- green to green products the concept will provide a way for adaptability and usability of green business.

One of the best ways to make the business more environmentally friendly is to practice green procurement. This involves sourcing goods and services that are produced and supplied in a sustainable fashion. A regular review in procurement policies should be ensured and the following issues should be properly analyzed i.e. manufacturing of product in a sustainable manner; assessment of materials or ozone-depleting substances; adjudging its viability of recycling or production from recycled materials, and above all, using renewable materials like bamboo for output of the product.

REFERENCES

Banerjee, S.B. (1998). Corporate environmentalism: Perspectives from organizational learning. Management Learning, 29 (2), 147-164.

Beckenbach, F. & Kahlenborn, W. (eds.) (2016). New perspectives for environmental policies through Behavioral Economics. Switzerland: Springer International Publishing.

Coddington, W. (1993). How to green up your marketing mix. Advertising Age, 61, 30.

Davis, J.J. (1992). Ethics and green marketing. Journal of Business Ethics, 11(2), 81-87.

Ehrlich, P. R., & Ehrlich, A. H. (1991). Healing the planet: Strategies for resolving the environmental crisis. New York: Addison-Wesley.

Fischer, K. & Schot, J. (1993). Environmental strategies for industry: International perspectives on research needs & policy implications. Washington D.C.: Island Press.

Gladwin, T. N. & Eidlin, R. (1992). Appraising the business impact of the Rio Conference. Total Quality Environmental Management, Autumn. doi:10.1002/tqem.3310020111.

Hawken, P. (1995). The ecology of commerce: A declaration of sustainability. New York: Harper Collins Publishers.

Kassaye, W. (2001). Green dilemma. Marketing Intelligence and Planning, 19 (6), 444-455.

Ottaman, J. A. (1993). Green marketing: Challenges and opportunities. Chicago: NTC Business Books.

Pearce, D. (1990). Environmentalism and business. In Rhys A. David (ed.), The Greening of Business. Book field, VT: Growing Publishing Co.

7

Natural Resources Management and Women Land Rights in India

INTRODUCTION

Land rights are integral ingredient of food security. A secured land rights is a vital part of an enabling environment that empowers women, promote inclusive economic growth and trim down extreme poverty. A proper Land rights can ensure the three recently endorsed Sustainable Development Goals (SDGs) that are; ending poverty, achieving food security, and empowering women. Indian women constitute a significant segment of the global agricultural labour force, but they are counting as the minority section so far as the agricultural landholders are concerned. Women not only hold less land than men counterpart but on an average, they hold very smaller and fragmented plots having inferior quality. This leads to a gender asset gap that has negative consequences for women, their families, their communities that leads to a global food security. When women have stronger rights and more access to land and productive resources, the production of crop per hector will increase. Secured land rights also lead to greater incentives to invest in the land which in turn will generate economic opportunities and leads to more sustainable farming practices. The land ownership of women's has also a positive correlation with the increase of income level, increase in the command of decision-making within the households, providing of better nutrition to child and improvised the status of quality educational attainment for girls.

The Indian Constitution provides equal rights to both men and women. Women's access to land is largely through inheritance and inheritance is governed by customs, which varies across regions and states. Aligned with the women land rights, the Hindu Succession Act enacted in 1956, to provide a comprehensive and uniform system of inheritance among Hindus and to address gender inequalities in the area of inheritance. Prior to this; the Hindu Women's Rights to Property Act, 1937 was in operation and it conferred rights of succession to the Hindu widow for the first time. Section- 14 of the Hindu Succession Act, 1956, declares, "Any property possessed by a female Hindu, whether acquired before or after the commencement of this Act, shall be held by her as full owner thereof and not as a limited owner." This makes women as absolute owners of their properties. However, many women are not aware of their rights; there is a misconception that women enjoy only limited rights over property. Further, the Act was amended in 2005 to give equal rights to women. The amended Act came into effect on September 9, 2005 and applicable to the various sections and castes of Hindus, apart from Sikhs, Buddhists and Jains.

In India, out of total cultivators almost one third are woman, but they own less than 10.34 percent of land, operating 12.8 percent of holdings, as per Agriculture Census, 2010-11, while 75 percent of female workforce, largely marginal or landless, depends on agriculture for survival. The average size of women's land holding is 0.93 ha, in comparison to 1.18 ha for male and 1.15 ha for all. Since independence, nearly 3.01 million hectares has been declared as ceiling surplus in the country. Of this nearly 2.31 million hectares has been taken over by the government and 1.76 million hectares distributed among 5 million beneficiaries, half of whom are Scheduled Castes and Scheduled Tribes. Besides, 7.26 lakh acres of government wasteland has been provided to the landless in the state. During the post land reforms period, not all intermediaries could be removed, because of non-availability of reliable records. The large-scale eviction of tenants also took place. No provision was made to record concealed tenancies. The survey of the legislative framework of Odisha taken over by the government confirms that 'land reforms policies have been based on the principle of redistributive justice and on arguments regarding efficiency with respect to land to the tiller, fixation of ceilings, prevention of fragmentation etc. The Odisha Survey and Settlement Act could not able to record the rights of tenants during settlement operations. Large scale transfer of land to adjacent farmers could not stop the fragmentation of land. And due to uneven terrain, farmers in western and southern Odisha neglected the consolidation of their landholdings.

The provision of settlement of government land to the landless is not at a "proactive" provision. Even "eligible" encroachers (normally referred to the landless) cannot "apply" to be regularised since of encroachment is considered illegal in the first place.

Similarly, identification and vesting of ceiling surplus land also has many loopholes. Big landholders not only avoid ceiling in the name of distribution of land among family members, they offer their waste or banjar lands as surplus land. Even the distribution of declared and vested ceiling surplus land among the landless has been very slow. The practice of transferring tribal land to non-tribal who uses a tribal pseudonym is very common. In many cases, the tribal have themselves turned into bonded labourers or underpaid agrarian labourers on their own lands.

Reflecting on the ground reality and statistical information identify huge gap between the statistical determination and the fact. This paper tries to assess the ground reality and reflection of the topic cited above. The context has been tested in three blocks of Nawarangpur (Tentulikhunti, Nandahandi & Dabugaon) and two blocks of Kalahandi districts (Bhawanipatna & M. Rampur).

The broad objectives of this paper are as follows:

- To Assess the level of awareness on women land right (FRA & Revenue land) with priority on convergences schemes in the study areas.
- Access & Control over land through implementation of FRA and Revenue land scheme by women.

The following methods and procedures have been undertaken in the study:

- Field Visit and individual interaction with target family.
- Focus group discussions with target community including FRC members.
- Key informant Collection from secondary sources, village profile and documentary evidences about the Status & Management procedures of IFR/CFR.

To have a basic understanding on the management of natural resources this paper tries to present the cases of Forest Rights and Revenue Land Rights.

UNDERSTANDING FOREST RIGHT ACT (FRA)

The very enactment of the historic Forest Rights Act, 2006 by the Indian Parliament in the country after 60 years of India's independence is a landmark constitutional reform. FRA aims at redressal of a numbers of problems arose due to the draconian Acts like Indian Forest Act, 1927 and Land Acquisition Act, 1894 which were used to evict the tribal's and the forest dwellers from their homes and shelters like goats and cattle. The Forest Rights Act, 2006 not only revived the tribal self governance regime in scheduled 5th area enforced by the Central PESA Act, 1996 but also it extended the provisions of the PESA even to the non scheduled area (whole State) empowering the Village Council, the Gram Sabha to decide over their fate and their resources which has been upheld by the Supreme Court, in the Niyamgiri case on 18th April 2013. All the State Machinery has now to accept that "Gram Sabha" as the lowest unit or form of "Government" having its own exclusive legislative, executive and judicial power and authority over its stipulated areas like any other forms of Government at Block, District, State and Central level.

Policies in India

Phases	Major Policies	Highlights
Phase- I 1947-1970	National Forest Policy (1952)	Commercial exploitation
Phase- II 1971- 1988	National Commission on Agriculture (1976);	Conservation through powerful legislation such as Wildlife Conservation Act & Forest Conservation Act.
	Forest Conservation Act (1980)	No place for forest dwellers and tribals in protection and management of local forest resources.
Phase- III 1988 Onwards	National Forest Policy (1988)	Based on three major components: Emphasis on participation of forest dwellers, Increasing access to forest products, Enhancing livelihoods.

CLASSIFICATION OF RIGHTS UNDER FRA 2006

Land Rights	No forest dweller can claim user rights over any forest land that he or she was not cultivating before 13 December 2005 and is not cultivating at present. Those who are cultivating such land but do not have documents to prove continuous land use can claim up to 4 hectares if they cultivate the land themselves only for their livelihoods. Those who possess government leases for forest land can claim user rights even if the land was taken by the Forest Department or is the subject of a dispute between the Forest Department and the Revenue Department. However, if those lands are re-conferred on an individual, a household, or a community, they cannot be sold or transferred to anyone except by inheritance
Community Rights	The FRA restores the forest dwellers' right to collect minor forest produce such as edible herbs and medicinal plants. But the forest dwellers cannot fell trees for sale. This also includes ownership and right to process and sell. The Amended Rules September 2012 even permits the gram sabha to issue transit permits. The law also recognizes the use of grazing grounds and water bodies by nomadic pastoralist communities.
Rights to protect and conserve	Until the FRA was enacted in 2006, only the Forest Department was entrusted with the duty of protecting forests. This legislation for the first time gives the forest-dwelling communities the right to protect and manage the community forest resource in their community forest within customary boundaries. It authorizes forest dwellers to conserve community forest resources by giving the community a general power to protect wildlife and forests. This is vital, as thousands of forest-dwelling communities are trying to protect their forests and wildlife against threats from forest mafias, industries, and land grabbers, most of whom operate in connivance with the Forest Department.

Relief and Development	The FRA states in Section 4(1) that "notwithstanding anything contained in any other law for the time being in force, and subject to the provisions of this Act, the Central Government hereby recognizes and vests forest rights in (a) the forest-dwelling Scheduled Tribes in states or areas of states where they are declared as Scheduled Tribes in respects of all forest rights mentioned in Section 3; (b) the other traditional forest dwellers in respect of all forest rights mentioned in Section 3." This is a powerful and unambiguous recognition of rights of forest dwellers and an unreserved vesting of such rights on them.

Source: Forest Rights Act 2006.

PROVISION OF RIGHTS UNDER FRA

The FRA lists the following as forest dwellers' rights:

- Right to hold and live on forest land as an individual or community and to cultivate land as a livelihood.
- Community rights such as cattle grazing on forest land.
- Right to collect, own, use, and dispose of minor forest produce that has been traditionally collected within or outside village boundaries by forest dwellers.
- Community rights to fish and collect other products from water bodies.
- Right to use traditional seasonal resources such as pastures and water bodies as nomadic or pastoralist communities.
- Community rights including tenures of habitat for primitive tribal and pre-agricultural groups.
- Right to reclaim any disputed land over which forest dwellers had user rights.
- Rights for converting to title leases or grants of forest lands issued by local authorities or state government.

- Rights of settlement and conservation of all forest villages, old habitation, un-surveyed villages and villages in forests.
- Right to protect, regenerate, conserve, or manage any community forest resource that the community has traditionally protected and conserved for sustainable use.
- Rights that are recognised under state law or laws of any autonomous district or regional council or rights that are accepted as rights of tribal people under any traditional or customary law of the concerned tribes of any state.
- Right to claim intellectual property rights over traditional knowledge related to biodiversity and cultural diversity.
- Any other traditional right enjoyed by the forest-dwelling Scheduled Tribes or other traditional forest dwellers, but excluding the traditional right of hunting or trapping of animals.
- Right to use forest land not exceeding one hectare to build schools, dispensaries, fair-price shops, communication lines, minor irrigation canals or other water bodies, vocational training centres, roads, community centres, and drinking water supply pipelines, subject to approval by the Gram Sabha (village assembly).

LAND LEGISLATION IN ODISHA & FOREST RIGHT ACT (FRA): THE BROAD PERSPECTIVE

The State of Odisha constituting only 4.73 of India's geographical area have around 7 percent of the total forest area of the country. While the reserved forest is spread over 26329 km constituting 45.28 percent. Protected forest spread over 15525 km 2 constituting 26.70 percent and the Un-classified forest is found in 16282 km constituting 28 percent of the total forest area which is 37 percent of the total geographical area of the State.

Govt. of Odisha while targeting the implementation of the historic Forest Rights Act, 2006 in the State referred the State of Forest Report, 1999 which stated that out of 46,989 villages in the State, there are 29,302 villages located in close vicinity of forest which are to be covered under FRA. The Government of Odisha also has estimated that out of 6420514 rural households, there are 1762342 ST households constituting 27.44 percent in the State. Besides, there is large number of Other Traditional Forest Dwellers in the State depending on the forest for their subsistence needs to be covered under FRA. Besides, Odisha has been the hub for the experiment of all the sensational issues in the country and always been in the limelight of media may be for its ample deposit of mineral and natural resources or for displacement, poverty, protest etc.

The central purpose of the Odisha Prevention of Land Encroachment (OPLE) Act, 1972 is to prevent unauthorized occupation of government land. It clearly lays down penalties for all instances of encroachment, to be followed by eviction. Through an amendment, during 1982 the state has recognized different types of encroachers on different types of lands .While all encroachers are required to be evicted from 'objectionable' lands, landless encroachers are legally entitled to be settled on up to one standard acre per family of 'non-objectionable' land (i.e. cultivable wasteland).

LAND ALIENATION FROM TRIBAL GROUPS

Odisha has a large tribal population (22 percent of total population, three times the average for India) and tribal land alienation by money-lenders has long been recognized to be a critical issue. Tribal people, with generally low educational and skill levels and limited access to formal credit markets, had little option but to seek credit at high rates of interest from moneylenders. In the event of default on loan repayments, moneylenders have tended to appropriate first tribals' forest produce, and later their land itself. Alienation of land held by members of Scheduled Tribes (ST) has been restricted by legislation as a matter of public policy. After Independence, the Constitution of India enabled state governments to make regulations restricting alienation of land by STs in Scheduled Areas.

In Odisha, Regulation 2 (1956) in Scheduled Areas provides that land held by a person belonging to a scheduled tribe cannot, without permission of the appropriate authorities, be alienated to a person not belonging to a scheduled tribe. The law also allows for a *suo moto* action by the Collector for restitution of alienated tribal lands. Section 22/23 of the OLR Act applies to prevent land alienation by tribals in non-scheduled areas. A less well-understood pattern is the administrative erosion of tribals' communal land rights through survey and settlement operations themselves.

The ownership of land in tribal areas has remained a complex issue for decades in most parts of India. Tribals living in forest areas are yet to receive legal entitlement over land in many areas they have been cultivating for decades. They face the constant threat of eviction and dispossession. Different categories of land and varied ownership, land use and management patterns make land resource management all the more complicated. In tribal areas, concentration of land in a few hands, illegal possession of land by the elite, passing off irrigated land as un irrigated land in land records and use of agricultural land for commercial purposes are some of the stumbling blocks in the individual's rightful access to land.

Land distribution at the time of Independence was extremely skewed. Fifty three percent of the land was held by seven percent of the landowners, whereas 28 percent of landowners with sub marginal and marginal holdings owned about 6 percent. The land distribution across the states was also quite skewed. Ceilings on land-holdings were essential because of three economic compulsions:

(1) there was strong evidence indicating an inverse size - productivity relationship, hinting that the aggregate production efficiency is hampered when land is held in large holdings;

(2) there was some evidence that large holders of land left large areas fallow thereby perpetuating uneconomic land use;

(3) a large proportion of the population were land-based poor who wanted land as an economic resource for their livelihoods. Thus, central policy-makers felt that surplus land could be distributed to the poor.

The general position in favour of land ceilings was based largely on providing social justice and equity and not on the grounds of increasing production and developing agriculture. Land ceiling was imposed to acquire surplus land from the big landlords and redistribute them among the landless.

Main Provisions and Impact of Land Legislation in Odisha

Name	Year	Provision	Impact
Odisha Estate Abolition Act	1952	Abolition of intermediaries. Vesting of all land rights in the state. Agricultural land less than 33 acres to remain with the intermediary for personal cultivation.	No provision protection for tenants. Eviction of tenants as the *zamindars* was allowed land, less than 33 acres, for personal cultivation. Abolition of intermediaries could not be completed until 1974.

contd...

Name	Year	Provision	Impact
Odisha Land Reforms Act (Amended in 1965, 1973 and 1974)	1960	Permanent, heritable and transferable rights in land for the tiller. Ban on leasing of land except under special conditions (in 1972). Under adverse possession, land in continuous cultivation for 12 years or more by a person other than its owner shall pass to the cultivator. Rent not to exceed one fourth of the gross produce. Ceiling on individual holdings at 33 standard acres-later reduced to 20 (in 1965), and to 10 standard acres (in 1972).	Delay in the enactment and actual implementation of the Act provided sufficient opportunities for large landowners to escape ceiling restrictions. By explicitly banning tenancy, the law is unable to address the problem of share-cropping. No provision was made to record concealed tenancies.
Odisha Survey and Settlement Act	1958	Different laws relating to survey, record-of-rights and settlement amended and consolidated into one uniform law.	Establishment of uniform though defective systems rights of tenants not recorded during settlement operations.

contd...

Name	Year	Provision	Impact
Odisha Consolidation of Holdings and Prevention of Fragmentation of Land Act	1972	Fragmentation of land declared illegal. First choice of transfer to adjacent farmer.	Little impact on land fragmentation. Occasional land sales but rarely to adjacent farmer. Consolidation of landholdings ignored by farmers in western Odisha because of undulating terrain.
Odisha Prevention of Land Encroachment Act (Amended in 1982)	1972	Unauthorised occupation of government land prohibited. Penalties on encroachers to be followed by eviction. The 1982 amendment for settlement of two (later amended to one) standard acres of 'unobjectionable' land (i.e. government wasteland) with 'eligible' beneficiaries (e.g. landless).	Disregard of the Act with widespread encroachment on both government and common lands, often by powerful groups. Penalties too low to act as a disincentive to encroachers. The 1982 amendment not a 'proactive' right-encroacher cannot 'apply' to be regularized as act of encroachment is regarded as illegal in the first place. Only Revenue Inspector can initiate regular-ization of rights.Considerable scope for rent seeking by revenue officials.

CRITERIA'S OF LANDS REGISTRATION IN WOMEN'S NAME

- After the death of husband, wife becomes a joint share holder of the deceased's land, along with her children.
- If a family has more land than the ceiling set by the government, the surplus land is recorded in the name of the wife/daughter to avoid ceiling restrictions.
- When there is no male heir in the family, daughters get the ROR transferred to their names.
- Unmarried women (those who could not marry and are living with their parents/brothers) get some land in their name. This does not come automatically, however, and often has to be contested.
- There are cases in which a woman's in-laws transfer the ROR in their daughter-in-law's name, such as in the event that an alcoholic man's parents believe that their son will sell off all their land.
- In some cases, when a woman marries a widower or divorced man, her parents generally insist that the man transfer some land in his new wife's name. This is done to ensure some economic security for the second wife in case the man marries for a third time while the second wife is alive. Another reason is that any children the man may have by his first wife might claim the entire property of the father leaving the second wife with no legal claim.
- Women's legal rights in land conflict with deep-seated social norms and customs, and are rarely recognized socially to be legitimate.

SOCIAL INCLUSION

Government poverty alleviation programmes are still far from the reach of these women as maximum number of women are yet to be fully aware of various schemes and programmes being implemented in their areas. Various reasons can be attributed to the same but some of the major cause are lack of effort at the government machinery to reach and circulate such relevant information in detail. Rather this has been an adhoc exercise at the people dealing such matters at the grassroots level. Women have relied more on their male counterparts and their opinion. Further it was found that the male counter parts of the Household have also applied for land under IFR or RL. The land record for the household is on the name of Joint awardees. Very few women possess Land Patta but do not have the physical possession over the land. Almost all community people possess PDS, BPL Cards.They face problems in getting adequate food grain as per their requirements. Fare price shops do not regularly provide service at the door steps though the Gram Panchayat has the responsibility to deal with such matter. Due to lack of strategic measures they have failed to deliver their services and people are suffering to get their food grains as per the government provision.

STEPS TO OVERCOME OBSTACLES IN THE PATH OF WOMEN'S PARTICIPATION

- Awareness about women's daily schedules.
- Sustained meetings and interactive sessions are barely necessary in these areas as by attending such meetings women would first of all be acquainted with the laws and legislations and then can spring into action and try to assert themselves. Accommodate women's request in terms of timing and location. Women are seldom able to visit geographically remote areas for the purpose of attending meetings.
- Analyze decision-making patterns within domestic units.
- It is often the male head of the domestic unit who is viewed as the decision maker and it may be so. It was found out that even though male members are in the front seat but women play vital role in the management of daily

activities and look after interest of children much more than men. Receiving independent input from women is essential in the context of land right as they would be more cautious.

- Recognize the different needs of different women.
- All women are not equal. Special attention need to be given to the situation of divorcees, female heads of households and widows.

MAJOR OUTCOMES

Women residing in Kalahandi and Nawarangpur districts in Odisha are the most disadvantaged groups who are illiterate as well as economically poor and face inconceivable challenges because of the society's discriminatory attitude towards them. When they are thrown out from their landholding rights illegally, it is really the most threatening act that must be interfered by the concerned governmental bodies such as the women and children affairs bureau. It is suggested that a provision of an effective legal aid for the Ethiopia women can be a voice for the voiceless.

In addition to the practical problems, the law also has a gap with respect to women in polygamous marriage. It does not specify how they can get their share from the matrimonial property. This legal gap could be filled by amending the relevant law. Significant knowledge already exists about women and land rights in India. Critical insights are also available on the inherent challenges women face in putting land rights into use; particularly in patrilineal family/social systems. New evidence is emerging from studies linking forest resources, farming, and livelihood and food security around women's land rights.

- **Recognize women as stakeholders**

The paper could bring out the idea in to surface that

importance of women's informed participation & access to water and land is a prerequisite for their overall development and assertion of right. Their active participation is key if their interest is to be taken into account. This participation also has to be in a meaningful way. They have to be informed of their rights and a support system has to be in place to help them defend those rights.

- **Ensure women's active participation in the processes**

This includes ensuring women in the community affected to be involved in the policy processes, from planning, to implementation, and to evaluation. This is not always an easy process and sensitive ways must be found in some communities to allow women to share their views and experiences openly, especially with strangers. Another way in which women in the community or organization can be encouraged to participate is to provide role models, such as appointing women as key project members and supporting them.

- **Obtain knowledge of the local situation**

NGOs and other organisations with motive and intent of fostering an enabling environment have to know whether women's access to land may be an issue; there is a need for an adequate assessment of the situation. The level of detail and complexity will depend on the local situation. However, if the situation does appear to have issues directly related to women's rights, then special measures may have to be taken to understand the potential implications. This can be done by obtaining feedback from women as well as male community leaders.

- **Provide opportunities for women's rights to be explicitly recognized**

If a land registration or information regarding rights to land is to be documented, then decisions need to be made as to: whose names will be documented and based on what evidence?

And how will these names be kept up to date? Many women opined that they have no idea on this aspect as this is generally the domain of their male members in family. The decisions made on such issues have to be acceptable to the recipient individuals/community to ensure the sustainability of the systems introduced.

- **Add the spouse's or partner's name to all legal documents concerning land rights, including any official register of land rights**

In case of family holdings, consent should be given by the spouse or partner. This helps to prevent fraud, adds security for the woman beyond family or legislative recognition and helps to ensure that both partners have idea on what their rights are.

- **Land administration institution/Revenue/forest departments of Govt. responsive and accommodating to women as well as men**

Responsive agencies are better able to serve the community especially in these areas as they have the double responsibility to explain the laws as well as the benefits under such laws. Apart from this they have to convince the individuals and communities on the process followed so that they are convinced about the transparency maintained. Such process can provide opportunities for inclusion.

- **Simplify registration procedures**

Women, especially poor women and female heads of households of these tribal and dalit dominated areas, are often unable to comply with excessive documentation requirements and they have shared the same during the course of the study. In their own feeling, such complexities make them uncomfortable to approach any authority and be clarified. They are also unlikely to represent their interests effectively and in a timely manner required in procedures. Female literacy is certainly an issue here and it could be easily marked during interaction with women SHGs and other groups. Efforts should be made to make women literate and understand the basic elements of land registration, documentation, schemes and programmes and the SC & ST department has to cover lot of ground in this regard.

RECOMMENDATIONS

- It should be taken into consideration that the illiteracy rate is much higher among women than men. Introducing training programmes and pictorial materials for the non-literate women population is essential in the study areas. Employ those forms of media that reach women in rural areas.
- Women should feel comfortable about being title holders. They should understand the rights, responsibilities and opportunities granting title to land and the potential changes and consequences that may bring in terms of their status (i.e. fees to be paid during transaction, possible tension with male members of their families, etc).
- The need based advocacy with the govt should be needed to provide financial support to FRC.
- The involvement of women should be ensured to place the claims (IFRs and CFRs) at DLC level.
- Awareness of women is a necessary condition for any development issue. The awareness will lead to empowerment which in turn acts as a base to achieve the desired goal of development.
- Women's experience and knowledge should be part of the initial community assessment. Facts pertinent to the project should be communicated to women by development professionals and women must have opportunity to voice their concerns without being

intimidated. Customary laws governing communities at large must be understood before implementing any programme.

- The attendance of women in different CBO meetings at the village level and GP level should be ensured, so that the women will own the programme on FRA or Revenue land.
- Project implementing organisations might be able to establish rapport with women's groups in the communities where women are not allowed to speak publicly in the presence of their male counterparts. It is however equally important that organisations have good understanding of the gender dimensions in the local situation.
- To create awareness among women regarding the FRA or Revenue Land, it is very essential to identify the specific area where the intervention is actually needed.
- The identification of women in the village is the first and foremost duty to form a forum to accelerate the FRA process.
- Meetings and interactive sessions are barely necessary in the project areas as attending such meetings by women would make them acquainted with the laws and legislations and then can spring into action and try to assert themselves.
- All VSS should be trained and empowered as CBO to make women more aware and participate in the process of women rights issues.
- All women are not equal. Special attention need to be given in case of divorcees, separated women, PWDs and widows.
- Women's access to land resources can only be sustainable if it is viewed by the community – both men and women – as legitimate. Project should strive to allocate resources

equitably and strive to ensure acceptance by the members of the community.

- Policy makers are expected to provide better understanding on the issues, status of the law, and any contradictions.
- Accept and acknowledge the issue where there is a problem regarding women's unequal access to land and associated resources.
- Women's lack of access or insecure access to productive resources is not always visible but is subject to transformation and modernization. Bringing the issue to the attention of appropriate authorities may not always be popular but may be considered part of the organisation.

CONCLUSION

Land is life blood of rural population. It is the main source of livelihood for men and women. Taking the importance of land into account, Constitution of India has afforded a legal protection for woman's right to equality with men and equal protection before the law. Thus women have equal right to own, administer and control property under the existing laws. Particularly, they have the right to access the land and control it equally as men. The revised laws of the country also uniformly recognize a woman's right to equal share of a common property, including land, upon divorce. Furthermore, women have an equal right to property inheritance too. However, this chapter describes that the law is not effectively implemented to its actual meaning in the tribal community because of various practical reasons. The main challenge to women's right to access and control over land in rural areas is the pessimistic attitude of the community towards women. The harmful practices are also prevalent among men who involve in various government systems at different levels. Moreover, women generally lack legal awareness on the breadth of their right to have access and control over the land. Therefore, legal awareness campaign should be undertaken by the concerned bodies for women. Moreover, women face challenges in enforcing their rights due to lack of information and awareness Thus, there should be organized state/central funded programmes which exclusively aims at the women's empowerment and enforcement of their land rights .

REFERENCES

Agarwal, Bina (May 2005). "Marital violence, human development and women's property status in India". World Development (Elsevier) 33 (5).

Agarwal, Bina (2002). "Are we not peasants too? Land rights and women's claims in India" (Pamphlet). SEEDS pamphlet series (The Population Council, Inc) 21.

Agarwal, Bina (January 2003). "Gender and land rights revisited: exploring new prospects via the state, family and market". Journal of Agrarian Change (Wiley) 3 (1-2).

Agarwal, Bina (October 1994). "Gender and command over property: a critical gap in economic analysis and policy in South Asia". World Development (Elsevier) 22 (10).

Allendorf, Keera (November 2007). "Do women's land rights promote empowerment and child health in Nepal?" World Development (Elsevier) 35 (11): 1975-1988

Besley, Timothy; Ghatak, Maitreesh (2010). "Property rights and economic development". Handbook of Development Economics (Development) (Elsevier) 5 (Chapter 68): 4525-4595.

Grown, Caren; Gupta, Geeta Rao; Kes, Aslihan (2005). Taking action achieving gender equality and empowering women (Task Force on Education and Gender Equality). London Sterling, Va: Earthscan. ISBN 1844072223.

Gupta, Geeta Rao (14 October 2009). "Guest column: when women farm, crops and economies grow". Truth about trade and technology.

Lastarria-Cornhiel, Susana (April 2005), "Gender and Property Rights Within Post conflict Situations - issue paper no. 12 (PN-ADB-672)."

Mc Creery, John L. (April 1976). "Women's property rights and Dowry in China and South Asia". Ethnology 15 (2).

Meinzen-Dick, Ruth S.; Brown, Lynn R.; Sims Feldstein, Hilary; Quisumbing, Agnes R. (August 1997). "Gender, property rights, and natural resources". World Development (Elsevier) 25 (8).

Raney, Terri (2011), "The State of Food and Agriculture 2010-11" (PDF), Women in Agriculture: Closing the gender gap for development (Food and Agriculture Organization of the United Nations, New York.

Steinzor, Nadia (March 2003). "Women's property and inheritance rights: improving lives in changing times - final synthesis and conference proceedings paper."

"The World's Women reports - World's Women 2000: Chapter 5-Work". United Nations Statistics Division.

8

Beggary and Economic Development: A Critical Economic Analysis

INTRODUCTION

Right to live with dignity is a fundamental right and it refers to the fundamental freedom and basic liberties without which men, women and children cannot live. The right to life is not merely confined to physical existence but it includes within its ambit the right to live with human dignity. It is not acquired as class inheritance, earned by socially approved behavior or assessed by one's industriousness or production. It is, instead, the companion to belief that all human beings are inherently worthy beings and the beggars as a class are not enjoying these rights at all. Beggars continue to remain the poorest of the poor and the most disadvantageous section of the society, living in such a deprived conditions that they are even unable to fulfill their basic needs of life. Beggars remain the most right-less people and in the eyes of the public, beggars are considered below the poor sections of society, attracting little public sympathy. Despite constitutional safeguards and State Legislative intervention to alleviate poverty, the socio-economic condition of beggars continues to deteriorate. Social and economic equality still remains a mirage for them. The importance of human dignity as the cornerstone of international human rights law has been confirmed by numerous international human rights instruments, like charter of the

United Nations 1945, which invoked the concept of human dignity in its preamble, again clearly linking human dignity and human rights. Even, the Universal Declaration of Human Rights, 1948, was a major step towards the emancipation of rights of human beings. In India, religious mendicants like Hindu 'Sanyasis' and Sadhus', Muslim 'Fakirs' and Darvesh's and 'Buddhist' monks present typical instances of vagrancy and beggary phenomenon. In many, perhaps most, traditional religions, it is considered that a person who gives alms to a worthy beggar, such as a spiritual seeker, gains religious merit. Similarly, many believe that Islam encourages begging, but it is a misconception that begging is supported by Islam. In fact, begging in Islam is considered a great sin and its practice is condemned and rejected in Islam

Begging has now become an occupation since no physical and mental effort is required to earn one's bread. This profession is based on the sympathetic behavior of the public towards the deprived people. No doubt, beggars are the needy persons, but up to some extent majority of them has adopted many strategies to collect more alms only to save themselves from physical works. Beggars are an inexorable part of our society and have to deal with this reality. Begging is a global phenomenon and not found in our society alone but rather it is found everywhere, in both developed and developing countries. Among beggars there are old people in ill health, the handicapped, the blind, retarded people, children, destitute and even the able bodied. A large proportion of beggars are the people who are unable to get on with life in a normal passion because of poverty, disability or other reasons. They can find no way out but to live on alms of others at the expanse of their dignity.

In India, the beggary laws are a throwback to the centuries old European Vagrancy Laws which instead of addressing the socio-economic issues make the poor criminally responsible for their position. Despite, the number of legislations passed by the different State Legislatures the menace of begging remains uncontrollable. These laws are not able to eradicate begging altogether as they completely criminalize a social problem borne out of poverty and destitution. Further, the definition of "begging" remains so vague that any person without visible means of subsistence could be apprehended for being suspected as a beggar. The act of begging constitutes a criminal offence in most Indian States and Territories with penalties ranging from two years to ten years imprisonment.

The problem of beggary is associated with the problems of poverty and unemployment, which is a social problem of great magnitude and grave concern in developing countries. Begging is a problem for society in as much as a large number of beggars means non-utilization of available human resources and drag upon the existing resources of the society. According to a recent survey by Delhi School of Social Work, there has been a phenomenal increase in the numbers of beggars in India. In a decade since 1991, their number has gone up by a lakh. There are some 60,000 beggars in Delhi, over 3, 00,000 in Mumbai according to a 2004 Action Aid Report; nearly 75000 in Kolkata says the Beggar Research Institute; 56000 in Bangalore according to police records. In Hyderabad, one in every 354 people is engaged in begging according to Council of Human Welfare in 2005. It is common to find beggars at rubbish dumb, roadsides, and traffic lights and under flyovers. The line that separates beggars from the casual poor is getting slimmer in a country where one in every four goes to bed hungry every night and 78 million are homeless. The survey reveals that begging as a livelihood wins over casual labour. For 96 percent the average daily income is Rs 80 more than what daily wage earners can make. Spending pattern also reveals a unique pattern: 27 percent beggars spend Rs 50-100 a day.

Most of the beggars preferred to move to the residential areas, markets and religious places of the district. Half of the beggars of the district preferred to go outside their own village or town for begging purpose and the proportion of native places and the other states of India recorded high in the urban areas as compare to the rural areas in which beggars mainly move to the surrounding villages (Khan, 2013).

An analysis made through a study that in Kadapa district of Andhra Pradesh the begging as a profession does encompass people from all the sections, including all age groups, sex, and caste groups. There is no significant difference across the caste groups in terms of number of beggars. Majority of the beggars have resorted to this profession not because of lack of economic resources, but due to some intra-family issues. Around 70 percent of the beggars hail from agriculturally potential areas. Regarding property possession, 74 percent of them have one or the other type of own property, and the value of such property shows a wide variation among them. Some have exceptional value of Rs.40 lakhs to 50 lakhs (Reddy, 2013).

The study based on primary source of data, collected through the field survey in the Aligarh district carried out during 2009 and altogether, 496 households of beggars were surveyed for the present study from the 70 villages of the district. Spatial analysis reveals the fact that the high level of demographic, literacy, employment, infrastructural facilities among rural beggars is witnessed in the peripheral parts of the district while, high level of per capita income is found in the central part of the study area (Khan, Menka, & Shamshad, 2013).

Begging in India is Rs. 200 crore industries. It was the data based information and after two years a survey conducted by Dr. Rafiuddin and got the findings that, on average a beggar earns Rs. 24,000/- per month in cities which is almost equal to a white collar job salary. There are instances of rich beggars in India for example a beggar was found with Rs.8,00,000/- in his garbage bag or a beggar with an insurance of Rs. 36,000/-

per year and though there are rich beggars the income is spread unevenly across the country (Rafiuddin, 2012).

While the poverty is real, begging is quite often carried out in organized gangs. Beggars have also been known to deliberately maim and disfigure themselves to get more money. Quite a bit of welfare work in India has been directed in reducing begging, including provided beggars with jobs, with varying degrees of success. The most common problem is that the beggars are so used to begging that they actually prefer not to work (Cook, 2016).

Global categories of street beggars and factors influence street begging in Nigeria has been analyzed by an article (Adedibu & Jelili, 2011).

By examining the consequences of begging and future aspirations of beggars to stop begging life in Central Tanzania; a cross-sectional study was conducted among 220 respondents composed of 130 beggars, non-beggars; 60 members of the focus group discussions and 30 key informants. Mixed methods and tools of data collection involving quantitative and qualitative approaches were used for data collection. Simple descriptive statistics were used for analyzing the data. The realized consequences of street begging were abusive languages from the public, harassments from municipal officials and police, harassment from fellow beggars; sun burn and cold during the nights, and sexual abuse were reported. Future aspirations of beggars in order to get rid of begging were getting capital to start small businesses, getting caregiver for themselves and their children, getting employment and getting accommodation. Counseling approach was recommended to help street beggars so as they may become assertive and hence become assets instead of liabilities to their families and society at a large (Namwata, Mgabo and Dimoso; 2012).

An analysis made in a study on the socio-economic

problems faced by beggars and governmental helps received by them as well as recommendation for upliftment of the socio-economic standard of their life in Aligarh district of Uttar Pradesh. It reveals that poverty, unemployment, lack of electricity, sanitation, potable water and proper housing, non-availability of ration card, lack of money for marriage of their daughters, various diseases, etc. are the main problems faced by the beggars. The help received from the government by the beggars merely are voter identity cards and ration cards. The study demonstrates that this section of population is the most poor among the poorest who are still thriving for one of the traditional basic need, that is food, what may be predicted about the status of the other remaining needs (Clothing and shelter). The new additive modern needs (health, education and recreation) are the heavenly dreams to them (Khan et., al; 2013).

OBJECTIVES

This chapter analyse the socio-economic profile of beggars and to find out the causes and factors that leads to their begging life. Further, the study tries to make a cause and effect analysis to the problem. In addition to this, some legal framework regarding begging has been analysed. The paper also presents the begging outcomes and its risk analysis. In this paper, a justification has been made in the point that no country, community, or economy will achieve its full potentials or will never meet up the challenges of the twenty-first century, when it's future leaders decides to beg in the street as their last resort. More specifically, this paper tries to give some remedial measures for improving the socio-economic conditions of the beggars.

METHODOLOGY

The methodologies adopted in this chapter were in the line of collection of data and analyzing them to reach its desired objectives. Here, the data were collected from the secondary sources and then by reviewing some literatures and some specific researches the outcomes have been placed in the paper. In addition to this, several Focus Group Discussions were conducted among the development practitioners and researchers on the topic.

Findings and Analysis

According to the Census data the following table and graph shows some bird-eye view of beggars in India in comparison to the national capital Delhi.

Beggars of India (As per 2011 Census)			
	India	**Delhi**	**%**
Male	221673	1343	0.61
Female	191997	844	0.44
Total	413670	2187	0.53

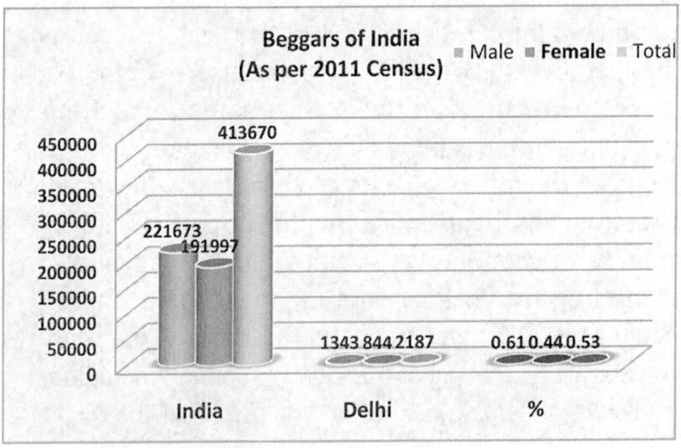

FACTORS RESPONSIBLE FOR BEGGARY IN INDIA

The problem of beggary, like any other social problem, is multidimensional. Its roots are found in the diversed patterns of its intertwined and interlocked social fabrics. It is very difficult to give specific reason or establish any reason for the situation of beggary, as is the case with a crime. There can be a set of causes that creates a situation of beggary. Some of the factors may be discussed below:

Physical Factor

In India, there is no adequate provision for treatment and social rehabilitation of blind, deaf, dumb or the persons with disabilities. In the absence of any reasonable alternative, such persons are constrained to beg.

Economic Factors

Economic factors which generally prompt people for begging. The three main causes may be poverty, job loss or lack of employment and business income:

- **Poverty**: One of the major factors that force people to adopt a miserable profession:
- **Unemployment**: But poverty alone cannot be held responsible because all those living in poverty are not used to beggary. Due to lack of education they are not eligible to be employed in any organised sector.
- **The productive business**: Because of easy profits and income from begging, some people can earn enough to make it as a career instead of doing honest labour. Not only that, many people make it as business and exploit others by investing some money in this business. There are group activities in large cities, which force many children to this job.

Social Factors

- Disorganized family: Family is part of the relationship of our society, which affect our pattern of behaviour and activities. Any interruption in our home state, especially in the case of a poor one leads to a breakdown of the family, which do arise in beggary.

- Lack of Parental Control: The parents do not have the industrial centre of control necessary for their children, but mothers also often go to factories to work. As a result, children can switch to energy in any direction. If they fall into bad company, they can develop love of travel, can lead to beggary.

Biological Cause: Among the biological causes may be addressed to illness, physical disability or mental disability and old age.

Disability or Illness: The physical disabilities such as blindness, deafness or acquired in the beginning had this effect on lot of people to beg as economic conditions of their families so as not to afford the maintenance of the disabled.

Lack of Spirit: There are people who suffer from mental retardment or insane and unable to earn any living and they are forced to beg.

Natural Calamities

Our physical environment may frustrate us drastically at times through famines, earthquakes, drought, cyclones or floods. Sometimes all these natural calamities cause serious damage to property and agriculture and compel people to leave their homes and compel them to take to begging to overcome pangs of hunger.

Psychological Factors

Sometimes, due to bad psychology of the individual cause beggary frustration, unwillingness to work and tendency towards isolation are important among these factors.

MAIN CAUSES OF CHILD BEGGARS IN INDIA

Here is a look at some of the main causes of child beggars in India:

1. Acute Poverty

Poverty is one of the main reasons that forces one to beg. A person who gets into begging seldom comes out of it. He involves his entire family in this profession. Young kids are especially considered good for this work and are thus forced to beg.

2. Lack of Education

Illiteracy is another reason for the rise in child beggars in our country. A person who is well educated would never get involved in this work and nor would he force his children to beg.

3. Unemployment

The problem of unemployment in India has also led to the rise in the number of child beggars. People here feel that there is no use of studying hard and acquiring degrees as they wouldn't get good job due to the problem of unemployment. This is why they involve their children in begging from the very beginning.

4. Refugee Community

Refugees who come from other countries because of different reasons find it hard to get a job and thus indulge in begging to meet their needs. They especially send their children for begging giving rise to child beggars.

5. Abandoned Children

Many children especially females are abandoned by their families immediately after their birth. Such children often get involved in begging, as it is the easiest means to get food and money.

6. Religious Sentiments of Indians

Indians are superstitious by nature. They seldom deny money to child beggars carrying bowl with the pictures of God and oil in it. It is said that donating money this way wards off evil. This is another reason beggars send their children to beg from street to street.

7. Begging Gangs and Rackets

Child beggars are considered a good catch by those who run begging rackets. Young children are said to be good for this work mainly because people feel pity looking at their innocent faces deprived of the basic necessities and offer them food and alms. Thus, these gang leaders look for more and more children to involve them in begging.

CATEGORIES OF BEGGARY

Beggars can be broadly categorised in the following categories:

- Professional/Hereditary Beggars- there are many nomadic tribes, which live by showing their talent of juggling, walking on the rope, singing, etc. These are professional beggars. Transgender can also be categorised in the type who get their livelihood by begging. These beggars do this from childhood and it is like a practice for them.
- Child beggars.
- Physically handicapped beggars/mentally retarded beggars.
- Diseased beggars-person suffering from chronic illness/ disease due to which he is unable to work and sometimes considered as economic burden on family are left out on their own.
- Religious mendicant's beggars-they have apparently renounced and became saint (sadhu, fakir) of a particular religion. They ask alms in the name of God and give their blessings in exchange.
- Employed Beggars- They do Beggary as a part time job.
- Temporarily unemployed beggars.

- **Able Bodied Beggars**– They find beggary easy and don't opt for any other job due to lethargy and unemployment.
- **Migrant Beggars–** Some of the poor section of rural area and other parts of country migrant to urban cities in search of employment but usually have to beg for their daily household expense.
- **Forced Beggars**– In urban areas beggars have formed associations. Some groups also abduct and deform children and force them to beggary and keep the money collected by them.

NEW INITIATIVES BY GOVERNMENT

The Centre is considering a scheme to provide shelter, health care and skill development training to the homeless and destitute to address the problem of beggary. Through the scheme prepared by the Ministry of Social Justice and Empowerment, the government aims at providing a whole range of basic services like food, shelter, health care, counselling and rehabilitation to destitute." Under the scheme, skill development training will be provided to the able-bodied destitute so as to facilitate their reintegration into the mainstream society and make them live a life with dignity." It will also encourage innovative interventions to strengthen the community-based approach towards rehabilitation of destitute with sensitization programmes etc., said a senior government official.

The problem of destitution and beggary is becoming a major concern and warrants urgent attention and intervention in view of the increasing numbers, especially the children and women. In order to ensure transparency and accountability in the implementation of the scheme, the details of every beneficiary would be maintained in a computerized database and linked with their Aadhaar number in due course of time.

According to a poverty estimation study by Oxford

University, UK, India is home to over 340 million destitute people and is the second poorest country in South Asia after strife-torn Afghanistan.

According to the 2011 Census, population of beggars and vagrants is about 4.13 lakh that includes 3.72 lakh persons under non-workers category and about 41,400 under marginal workers category.

The Ministry of Social Justice and Empowerment, during 1992-1993 to 1997-98, had implemented a scheme for the prevention of beggary under which financial assistance was provided for establishment of work centers in the existing beggar homes for providing vocational training and technical education.

The scheme was discontinued from the year 1998-99 due to moderate demand from the state governments. There is no ongoing comprehensive central scheme directly related to protection, care and rehabilitation of destitute persons. However, the centre is implementing a number of programmes for the welfare of vulnerable groups.

Under the new scheme, government would provide financial assistance to rehabilitation centers run directly by states and Union Territories which will ensure availability of basic amenities such as food, shelter, clothing and health care are available to the destitute and homeless, The centres will arrange for facilities to provide vocational training to able-bodied destitute above 18 years so as to enable them to start income generating activities on their own or get gainfully employed in some sector. Also, in order to monitor the implementation of the scheme, the states and UTs may set up State Advisory Committees or Boards.

BEGGARY AND ECONOMIC GROWTH

Beggary does not denote only misery and appalling conditions. It is an economy in itself. In Mumbai, there are estimated to be 100,000 beggars. This population grows because every couple breeds at least six children because that really means eight workers on the road. The smaller the child the merrier it is for the parents because there is a better chance of a two-year-old being given money than an adult. There is also a definite preference for girls as their presence evokes a more sympathetic response from the public. Now, it has been estimated that a beggar could earn anything between Rs 50 to Rs 100 a day. It may be an exaggeration since there are contractors or intermediaries here who probably give these people not more than Rs 20.

Now-a-days, beggars have stopped accepting anything less than a rupee and you often have to pay two rupees to the beggar who wipes a dirty cloth over your car. At Rs 20 a day, they rake in Rs 20 lakh (Rs 2 million) all put together, which means Rs 6 crore (Rs 60 million) a month or Rs 72 crore (Rs 7.2 million) a year. Moreover, if we sum it across the rest of the country, the amount will top at least Rs 1,000 crore (Rs 10 billion). This money is tax-free and almost always transacted in one rupee coins. We are excluding the rag pickers and people in the charity homes and orphanages, which are more organized. We are also excluding the trading of these coins by these beggars in areas where there are shortages. Now, the Rs 1,000 crore (Rs 10 billion) is always spent and never saved. Hence, it has strong backward linkages, since it supports the petty retailer and provides a steady income to 150,000 to 200,000 retailers (assuming an income of Rs 5,000 a month for a vendor) in the form of tea stalls, small eateries, fruit vendors and so on. The beggar economy hence forges link with the informal sector of the economy and promotes growth and above all employment.

Beggars are a vital part of the economy, which is not supported by the government and has society indirectly funding their existence. In fact, quite curiously, if we do go along with the estimated figure of Rs 50 a day collected by a beggar, then the total amount of transfer payments made to this class by society would be around Rs 2,000 crore (Rs 20 billion) at the national level, which is around 5 per cent of the total central government subsidy bill. Therefore, as the value of poverty in our country has ironically gone up, it needs less government support and sustains employment of several others. It does what the government is unable to do on its own as it always crying over the fiscal deficit. Surely, there is a lot to think over when you part with those coins the next time.

Whenever we talk about beggar, this always link us the problem of poverty. It has been an important issue in Vietnam for years. Currently, there are still a large number of people living in "social bottom" life. This is particularly noticeable in the background of strong stratification when the income gap between rich and poor start becoming bigger and bigger. The process has a vibrant character; the poor are getting poorer and the rich even richer. Moreover, it can create some illegal acts in humanity.

LEGAL FRAMEWORK RELATING TO BEGGING

The Indian Constitutional provisions have equally played a rightful role for shaping the concept of human rights into a reality. The framers of the Constitution were aware of the significance of human dignity and the framers showed an uncompromising respect for it. The Preamble, the Fundamental Rights, the Fundamental Duties and the Directive Principles of State Policy are the concrete steps towards the realisation of human rights. Whereas, the basic objectives have been defined in the Preamble to the Constitution of India, more emphasis has been laid on the protection of human freedoms and liberties in the Fundamental Rights (Part-III of the Constitution) and Directive Principles of State Policy (Part-IV of the Constitution). All these provisions enumerated in the

Constitution of India epitomize the collective will and aspirations of all men, women and children of India, but in reality, the study suggests that the beggars are not enjoying any such human rights, freedom and liberties.

The subject of destitution and beggary is not mentioned in either Central or State list. However, as per entry nine of the state list in the seventh Schedule of the Constitution, "relief of the disabled and unemployable" is a state subject. On the other hand, as per entry 15 of the Concurrent List, "vagrancy" is mentioned which is a variation of beggary. Kidnapping or maiming a minor for the purpose of begging is treated as an offence under section 363-A of IPC. Further, Section-24 of Juvenile Justice Act, 2000 prohibits employment of juvenile or child for begging. Section-144 of the Indian Railway Act, 1989 stipulates prohibition of hawking and begging. At present, 20 states and 2 UTs have either enacted their own anti-beggary legislations or adopted those enacted by other states. These anti-beggary laws are mostly based on the Bombay Prevention of Begging Act, 1959 which criminalizes the act of begging and any person found involved in it can be arrested without warrant.

With a large number of destitute in the country, the economy has to bear a huge load with very small or no contribution to the gross domestic product and it leads to wastage of human potential.

"Apart from economic burden, beggary causes other social problems such as drug abuse, trafficking, organised crime, child-related crimes etc. Therefore it needs redressal both by the government and civil society through concerted efforts to arrest potential criminal activities like organised begging, trafficking of drugs etc."

I. Constitutional Provisions

According to the Constitution, to make provisions for beggars comes under the jurisdiction of State government.

Under Article-214 of Constitution, the meaning of right to life is expanded to right to life with dignity. Article- 457 guarantees compulsory free education until 14 years of age. However, it is very regretful for that these provisions are not yet properly implemented since we have 3.7 lakh beggars in India.

II. State Legislations

There is uniform law in India to deal with beggary, though many states have passed their own laws. There are 22 different laws in different States and UTs, which are mainly the extension of Bombay Prevention of Beggary (BPB) act, 1959. BPB criminalizes beggary in Mumbai and Delhi. Section-2 of BPB act defines begging and Section-6 has provision for punishment of 3 to 10 years of jail for begging. The punishment of employing person for begging is 1-3 years of jails under Section-11 of the act. The law prima facie looks unconstitutional. It gives the provision of punishing the victim. It is applicable in Mumbai and Delhi, which are the two most important cities of India. This may be due to the presence of large number of beggars and rackets in these places but to punish the victim is not the right way to solve any problem.

Criminalizing forced beggary and prohibiting child beggars seems to be logical but criminalizing beggary with heavy punishment is not. In the BPB act, the ambit of 'Begging' is extended by including "singing, dancing, fortune telling, performing or offering any article for sale", which is not only restrict them to get their livelihood from begging but also from legitimate means.

III. Other Laws Related to Beggary

Under IPC, provision for punishment for kidnapping or maiming a minor for the purpose of begging is given in Section-363A. The Indian Railways Act, 1941, prohibits begging in railway premises and trains. But the implementation of this law does not seem to be effective as many beggars can be found on various railway premises and trains.

Blanket law for decriminalizing of beggary should come into effect. Various states have different laws with several loopholes. The Persons in Destitution (Protection, Care and Rehabilitation) Model Bill, 2016, which is a pending bill that should be passed, which have provisions of rehabilitation and rescue of beggars. Government spends a lot of money to eradicate poverty, but no proper strategy and implementation is followed to do so. It is the need of hour to have a better and practical intervention strategy to be implemented in whole country to fight with poverty.

IV. Laws against Child Beggary in India

Child beggary is not only a direct attack on the right of the child but also a direct attack on country being labeled as a developing nation. Every part of our legal system has stood against child beggary and has stated provisions related that. The Bombay Prevention of Begging Act, 195 has criminalized begging and has made provisions that are relevant to children between the age group of 0-18. Under this act, a child is a boy who is below the age of 16 and a girl who is below the age of 18 years of age and people found guilty under this law is deemed to be punished for the minimum time-period of 1 year and a maximum time gap of three years in Beggars Home. Moreover, this act also stands against those who exploit the children to beg for alms for the similar time-period in prison. Moreover, the Clause-(d) of the act has mentioned the definition of beggar as "having no visible means of subsistence and wandering about or remaining in any public place in such condition or manner makes it likely that the person doing so exists by soliciting or receiving alms". However, the definition proved to be a sham when the Delhi Government's social welfare department conducted a survey stating most of the beggars to be "able-bodied and educated." The poor children are often witnessed in a highly packed road thus; The Traffic Police Notification (under the Motor Vehicles Act) imposes a fine on motorists who give money to beggars. The Delhi Traffic Police has issued a direction to all motorists in the capital not to give alms to beggars at traffic signals, as this hinders traffic flow, sometimes even causing accidents. The fine for a first violation is Rs 150; the second time around it is Rs 300.

V. Anti-Begging Laws in India

In India, there is no central law, which penalizes begging. Although, 22 states (including few Union Territories) have their anti-begging laws. The Act, which functions as the derivative figure for all the state anti-begging law is Bombay Prevention of Begging Act, 1959. The act prescribes penalty of more than three years of jail in case of first conviction for begging and person can be ordered to be detained for ten years in subsequent conviction.

All offences under this act are to be tried summarily except those under Section-11 of the act, which penalizes the act of employing or causing persons to beg or use them for the purposes of begging. The Act elaborates in the aforesaid section that if any person employs or causes any other person to solicit or receive alms, or whoever having the custody or charge of the child, connives or encourages, their employment or the causing the child to solicit or receive alms or uses another person as an exhibit, shall be punished for imprisonment for a term up to three years but which shall not be less than one year. Section-24(1) of the Juvenile Justice (Care and Protection of Children) Act, 2000 provides that whoever employs or uses any juvenile or the child for the purpose of begging or causes any juvenile to beg, can be imprisoned up to three years and shall be liable to fine. Those who abet begging are also liable for the same punishment. Section 363A of Indian Penal Code (IPC) provides for punishment for a person who kidnaps or maims a minor for purposes of begging. Unauthorized vending/hawking and begging in trains and Railway premises is an offence under the provisions of Section-144 of the Railways Act, 1989.

VI. Legality of Bagging

According to the Bombay Prevention of Begging Act, 1959, the provision not only criminalizes the begging in the Mumbai but also in various metropolises such as Delhi.

However, last year, the Delhi High Court in a landmark judgment has held the Act as unconstitutional in Delhi, on the grounds of violation of Article-14 and Article-21 of the constitution restoring the rights of persons who have no other means of sustenance but to seek alms. The court has acknowledged that the application of the anti-beggary act has largely been arbitrary, leading to the detention the poor who may not be engaged in begging, but could be people who have "fallen through the socially created net" – they could be homeless, poor persons living with disabilities, transgender persons, migrant or sex workers.

About four lakh beggars of India must have heaved a sigh of relief with the Delhi High Court ruling that seeking alms is not a crime, even as blasting the government for turning a blind eye toward the most vulnerable and downtrodden section of society. The unprecedented decision to strike down as many as 25 provisions of a draconian anti-beggary legislation also means instant freedom for hundreds of panhandlers being prosecuted and dumped into dungeons for months on end.

PROBLEMS FACED BY BEGGARS IN INDIA

Beggars in India face numerous problems. Some of these problems are severe and can even be beyond our imagination. Some of the main problems faced by beggars in India are given below:

1. Absence of Food and Shelter

Beggars in India lead their entire life living on the roadside. Their whole family sits on the roadside during the day begging the passers-by for food and money and sleeps on the footpath or underneath a tree near the same place as it grows dark. Food, clothing and shelter are the basic needs of the human beings and beggars are denied even these basic needs. Such is the plight of these poor people.

2. Deprived Hygiene

Living on the roadside, the beggars do not have access to good quality food; safe drinking water as well as water which is clean enough to bath or good enough for sanitation purpose. They do not bathe for days and roam around in the same clothes for weeks without washing them. They, thus, suffer from poor hygiene.

3. Underprivileged Health Conditions

Poor hygiene leads to poor health condition. Besides, these people do not have proper shelter and are faced with adverse climatic conditions such as strong heat wave, heavy downpour and chilling cold. Eating healthy food is beyond question for them. All this has a severe impact on their health and leads to various illnesses.

4. Lack of Medical Facilities

When these poor people fall ill they do not even have access to good medical facilities to get themselves cured. They cannot afford the enormous fee charged by the private doctors. While some of them don't visit the doctors at all and wait for the condition to get better on its own others go to the government dispensaries or hospitals that are over-crowded with patients and lack proper patient care.

5. Illiteracy

Illiteracy is the main problem. Beggars are mostly illiterate and do not make any effort to send their children to school either. Instead of providing education to their kids, they force them to beg on the street. This gives rise to the illiteracy as well as crime rate. Education can change a person for good but these people do not understand this.

6. Begging Rackets

There are gangs that force people to beg. They kidnap young children or give a ransom to the poor families in their exchange and engage them in begging. These gangs divide areas and send beggars for begging in their respective areas. At the end of each day, they take away a substantial amount of cash and kind collected by the beggars. The beggars are helpless in this case. The worst part is that these gang leaders even make these beggars handicapped to invoke pity of the public and get more alms.

INDIA PLANS FOR ERADICATION OF BEGGING

India is making efforts to eradicate begging, but it is going to be an uphill task to resettle over 4 lakh beggars who spread across the country. In fact, beggars had been removed from Hyderabad, ahead of the visit of US president Donald Trump's daughter Ivanka Trump who attended the three-day Global Entrepreneurship Summit (GES). The Union Government is now charting a comprehensive effort to address the issue. The Ministry of Women and Child Development is implementing a centrally sponsored Integrated Child Protection Scheme (ICPS) for Children in Need of Care and Protection (CNCP).

As per Juvenile Justice Act, a child who is found working in contravention of labour laws for the time being in force or is found begging or living on the street is included as a "child in need of care and protection". Under ICPS, financial assistance is provided to the State Governments/UT Administrations for inter-alia, undertaking a situational analysis of children in difficult circumstances, for setting up and maintenance of various types of Child Care Institutions (CCIs). The scheme provides institutional care through CCIs.

As a rehabilitative measures in these CCIs, children are provided age appropriate education either within the institution or outside in a formal education system through convergence with other schemes and programs of the Government or Civil Society. The Scheme also provides for family based non-institutional care through adoption, sponsorship and foster-care.

As per available information, 20 States and 2 Union Territories have enacted their own anti-beggary legislation or adopted legislations enacted by other State/UTs. The challenge is to rehabilitate 4,13,670 beggars - 2.2 lakh males and 1.91 lakh females. According to a recent survey by NDTV reported that West Bengal with 81,244 beggars topped the list followed by 65,835 in Uttar Pradesh, 30,218 in Andhra Pradesh, 29,723 in Bihar and 28,695 in Madhya Pradesh. Incidentally, in Assam, Manipur and West Bengal female beggars outnumbered their male counterparts. Moreover, the union territories recorded the least number of beggars.

INITIATIVE FOR REHABILITATION OF BEGGARS

The Union Government is mulling over a new centrally-supported initiative for the rehabilitation of beggars as local self government bodies in India have failed to implement schemes for the same. Recently a few municipal corporations in Maharashtra including Pune Corporation had launched 'beggar free city' campaign. However, the campaign was abruptly concluded and hardly any beggar was rehabilitated across the state. The Pune Corporation claims that it has rehabilitated 16 of 479 beggars that were identified in the city.

BEST PRACTICES TO END MENACE OF BEGGARY

- In Bihar, Mukhyamantri Bhikshavriti Nivaran Yojna was launched to protect and promote the rights of beggars by ensuring their care, protection, development, socio-economic and cultural empowerment through enabling policies and programmes.
- The Government of Odisha has adopted various measures to identify beggars, provide them alternative remedy like houses, insurance coverage, Aadhaar and ration card, healthcare facility, giving them training for vocational skills for wage or self-employment.
- Few Municipal Corporations in Maharashtra including Pune Corporation had launched 'beggar free city' campaign.

APPROACHES OF ODISHA GOVERNMENT TO COMBAT BEGGARY

The Odisha government has identified 6,390 beggars across the state. In this context, the state government is implementing a special scheme 'Sahaya' to identify the destitute new, counsel them, do their trait analysis and give them skill development training free of cost before giving them incentives in kind to set up their own business and become self reliant. The scheme 'Sahaya' is meant for protection, care and rehabilitation of beggars and through this scheme government has planned to provide alternate livelihood to 2,886 beggars. Government has identified beggars in all 30 districts of the state. Cuttack district topped the list with 1,060 beggars followed by Balangir (708), Mayurbhanj (485), Sundargarh (467), Ganjam (458), Nuapada (288), Sonepur (280), Sambalpur (223), Bhadrak (220), Kalahandi (214) and Koraput (200). Other districts have beggars less than 200. Deogarh district has the least number of beggars that is only 16. Other districts including Boudh (19), Malkangiri (21), Kendrapada

(22), Jharsuguda (41) and Jagatsinghpur (53) have less number of beggars in the state.

Sahaya, the scheme for protection, care and rehabilitation of beggars aims at providing comprehensive rehabilitation support to all the target groups. The rehabilitation plan of beggars will include, among other things, homestead land, houses, insurance coverage, Aadhaar card, ration card, healthcare, developing skills for living by restoring their psychological strength, confidence and giving them training in vocational skills for wage or self-employment. It will assist parents of beggars, pre and post matric scholarship, skill development training, self-employment kit, Self-Help Group, rehabilitation centers and marriage incentives and support for daughter of beggars. Beggars or destitute roaming around the streets seeking alms may no longer be a common sight in Bhubaneswar or other cities across the state. The Odisha Government has planned to make the whole of the state beggar and destitute free. To find a permanent solution to the problem, the government has decided to launch an array of training and skill development programmes to rehabilitate beggars and destitute and make them an integral part of the state workforce.

The State Department of Social Security and Empowerment of Persons with Disabilities (SSEPD), the nodal agency entrusted with the task of enforcing the ban, is persuading them to become a productive part of the state labour force to shun the age-old practice of begging. The idea is to not only remove beggary from the cities but also devise proper planning to harness their energy in a more productive manner.

Some of the identified training areas which could be availed by the beggars or destitute to become self-dependent include carpentry, tie and dye, craft works, stone carving, leather art training, spray painting, welding, diary making training, gem cutting, leather works, videography and photography, electrical training, garment designing, cooking/catering, horticulture, spinning and welding, book binding and many others.

The state government has also planned to award those beggars who want to return to the mainstream. The norms for the scheme read, "To ensure a long-term incentive and support the beggars, they are required to be awarded incentives. The beggars returning to mainstream society will be awarded an incentive support of Rs 50,000. The award will be placed in fixed deposit in the name of the person in destitution for a minimum period of three years." Beggars, as per norms, would also get self-employment kits depending upon their trade requirement to enable them to start their own business. The State District Social Security Officers (DSSOs) would be given the responsibility of distributing the kits in consultation with the SSEPD department.

In Bhubaneswar, the survey to identify the beggars and destitute has already been carried out. The maiden counseling session of 30 beggars in the first phase has also been held in presence of SSEPD Department, NCSCDA and Patita Uddhar Samiti wherein the participants were informed about the scheme and its benefits. Similarly, in Sambalpur, around 37 beggars are reported to have undergone training from different blocks and are now ready to start their career as a small-time entrepreneur.

CONCLUDING REMARKS

The vicious circle of poverty goes in the same way with the viscous circle of beggary. Child beggary can be well compared with the contagious disease which is difficult to eradicate from its roots. As every child has a dream to go school, the children asking for alms too has the same dream. In the 86th Amendment Act, 2002 Right to Education is added in the constitution of India where in Section 21(A) envisages free and compulsory education and a fundamental right to all the children between the age group of six to fourteen years. Many parents and children are not even aware of the role of education in one's life. Giving a two-rupee coin does not fulfill the necessity of a child but it encourages them to continue their usual habit of living and giving them belied hopes to a good life. Moreover, it also gives hope to the extortion mafia's to expand their business. Child beggary in India not only impedes the country's progress towards the development but also is acting as a parameter to determine the poverty, illiteracy and under development level of the nation.

Begging is a cause of concern for the society. It is an intractable challenge for young children are involved in this activity. In India, the number of child beggars is huge. At an age when these young minds should be nurtured with love and care, given good education and involved in healthy activities, most of them are deprived of all this and are forced to beg for their livelihood. While beggars are usually found at the traffic signals, in front of the temples and other such places, some of them also roam around from street to street to beg for alms, money and food. These are the worst kind of beggars as they intrude the residential areas and disrupt peace.

With the nation aspiring for achieving world standards in every field socio-economic measures need to curb the begging problem in India. The solution calls for a comprehensive programme and reorientation of the existing programmes. Philanthropic approach to beggar problem should be replaced by therapeutic and rehabilitative work.

As per the above facts we observe that people with no fixed income or even see beggary is a business. This is a problem whose solution is the mass of the nuance that require special attention. In Vietnam, beggary is still legal, even though the government is concerned about the issues has taken initiative to prevent children from going on the street and begging for money. By considering all the pros and cons of the situations, it can be concluded that solving this problem is most important to overcome the systemic crisis in the country, to carry out social policies that would be purported to ensure normal living conditions for the majority of the population, especially the so-called most unprotected.

Thus, child beggary is still a burning problem in India and we must combat the evil, which is spreading its wings day by day. Pandit Nehru had once said that children are the future of the nation and the future is at stake. We need to extirpate the social evil of child beggary and put up those laws and regulation, which would prove to be fruitful for the future of our children and for our nation. Even though the government is taking measures to stop it and many NGOs have been formed to eradicate this problem, nothing visible has been done yet.

Suggestions and Recommendations

Begging has grown at a significant rate in India. It is estimated that half a million people in India are beggars. The government, varied organizations, activists' claim that many measures have been taken to abolish begging and it has been successful to a certain extent. But the trend of begging still continues. Indians are very orthodox, god-fearing and have a religious frame of mind. This compels them to do charity and encourage this process.

However, as the citizens of India, it is our moral responsibility to stop giving alms to eliminate this menace. It may be irrational not to give money to a little child begging on the street, but this is the prelude to prevent the menace of begging. If people affirm not to give a single penny to any beggar, irrespective of their need, there will be a psychological impact on the beggars. The Government should continue with its poverty alleviation schemes and make India a better place to live in.

In Indian society, especially Hindu castes, the poor beggars belonging to Brahminical caste are treated differently to those of dalit and lower caste beggars. While 'Yachakas'(the Brahmin people asking for alms) are given food and money to attain virtue (Punya), the dalits are often abused and sent away most of the times. This discrimination should also be addressed and such evil must be stopped. As dalits and lower castes comprise more than those belonging to upper castes, there is a need to address the problem from caste point of view. Prohibition of caste system should go hand in hand with the upliftment of beggars in the society.

Rehabilitation of Beggars

Begging has grown at a significant rate in India. It is estimated that half a million people in India are beggars. The government, varied organizations, activists' claim that many measures have been taken to abolish begging and it has been successful to a certain extent. But as the citizens of this country, it is our moral responsibility to stop this menace and the best way is to stop giving alms. Meanwhile, let the government continue with its poverty alleviation schemes and make India a better place to live in.

Following suggestions may be taken to rehabilitate beggars:

- **Poverty Eradication:** Priority should be given to eradication of extreme poverty. Though many people take to begging owing to poverty, it has become a menace. Of late, begging has become part of an organized crime.
- **Rehabilitation:** Small shelters have to be made and they need to be imparted skills that would help them for economic self reliance. They should be made to earn their livelihoods by working and not begging. The government and charitable organizations should look after people who are aged and physically challenged.

- **Vocational Training:** The government should provide necessary vocational training to rehabilitate them. The expenses incurred should be borne by the government. A government funded organization should be constituted and personnel trained to oversee the rehabilitation programme. Beggars who are willing to work should be trained according to their ability, health and talent. They should be given medical care, food and other amenities. Necessary steps should be taken by the government to collect contributions from donors by allowing tax rebate.
- **Intensive Effort:** Social issues associated with begging are drug trafficking, criminal activities and sexual exploitation of children. As part of the rehabilitation programme, the corporation has collaborated with a voluntary organization towards providing food, clothing and medicines. To reduce the economic burden, the government should seek the aid of voluntary organizations. However, the activities of the voluntary organizations should be monitored and evaluated.
- **Need for Aid Agency:** The rehabilitated should be provided free medical diagnosis, financial support and ration to the beggars. Slums may come up in cities and rehabilitation should be carried out in a judicious manner.
- **Create Awareness:** People should discourage beggars. Begging makes a stride because of generosity of the people. Awareness programmes need to be conducted for the poor to help them realize how shameful it is to beg.

Corrective Approach for Rehabilitation

By treating beggars simultaneously as criminals and as those in need of help, different State Governments have failed in their duty to reintegrate them into society. Punitive approach incriminates them again, and the punishment for repeated offences is higher extending to detention for an indefinite period of time. India's policy-makers must develop a consistent and humane approach towards begging, which focuses not on penalizing but on rehabilitating them. The model bill marks a shift towards a more rehabilitative approach, but continues to perceive ostensible poverty as indicative of begging, and allows indefinite detention and the involvement of police in certain circumstances.

Way Forward

Food, clothing and shelter are the basic needs of human being. The right to life is guaranteed in any civilized society. That would take within its sweep the right to food, the right to clothing, the right to decent environment and a reasonable accommodation to live in. It remains a hard reality that the State has not been able to ensure even the bare needs of the right to life to all its citizens. People beg on the streets not because they wish to, but because they need to. Begging is their last resort to subsistence; they have no other means to survive. Begging is a symptom of a disease, of the fact that the person has fallen through the socially created net.

As India is a welfare state, it is the responsibility of the government to devise policies for all its citizens to achieve the wholesome life. India is also part of the International Covenant on Civil and Political Rights (ICCPR) that has a provision for right to living with dignity. Lack of any concrete policies to deal with the issue of beggary and homelessness is inconsistent with that provision.

In the light of the foregoing discussion and the conclusion thereof, the following suggestions are made to prevent the menace of begging and giving beggars a dignified life:

- The real solution is to recognize and combat structural injustices in society and expand livelihood options in the national economy. Nevertheless, in the process, it is vital to envisage a legal system that does not persistently exclude the most marginalized section from the development process.

- There should be a clear-cut division of jurisdictions, responsibilities, and financial resources between the national and sub-national administrative systems following a general agreement and consensus on the broad strategies for poverty reduction based on actual data and expert/technical considerations. It is, therefore, necessary to reorient the institutional arrangements at the sub-national level to include provisions for adequate representation of all sections and interests of populace at the grass-roots level, particularly women and other weaker, poor and vulnerable sections of the society for whom the strategies for poverty reduction are being evolved. It is also necessary that the politico-administrative institutions at the sub-national level have access to the necessary technical help, expertise and administrative support to plan, modify, and formulate their strategies for poverty reduction at their own level in accordance with their specific requirements and local considerations.
- In most of the existing acts, for example Section 2(1) of BPBA, 1959 and Section 2(a) of JKPBA, 1960 the definition of "Begging" provided therein seems to be too vague, that any person without visible means of sustenance could be apprehended for being suspected as a beggar. Further, the definition of the term is so wide that persons managing livelihood through their individual skills could easily be roped in. Therefore, it is suggested that the definition may be modified as:

  (i) Soliciting or receiving alms in public place,

  (ii) entering on any premises for the purpose of soliciting or receiving alms;

  (iii) exposing or exhibiting, with the object of obtaining

or extorting alms, any sore, wound, injury, deformity or disease whether of a human being or animal;

(iv) allowing oneself to be used as an exhibit for the purpose of soliciting or receiving alms; but does not include soliciting or receiving money or food or gifts for a purpose authorized by law, or authorized in the manner.

In a country like India where alms giving still continues to be a religious practice, the definition of begging that includes a varied behavioral patterns which people in general not only tolerate but also support as part of their traditions, needs to be reviewed.

- India's beggary laws are a throwback to the centuries old European vagrancy laws which instead of addressing the socio-economic issues make the poor criminally responsible for their position. India as a nation needs to think of its begging population and with the nation aspiring for achieving world standards in every field, socio-economic measures are needed to address the begging problem. The de-humanizing process of detention, trial and imprisonment of beggars needs to be scrapped. Thus, a new Act needs to be framed incorporating changes on the judicial procedure, living standard in certified institutions, rehabilitation and vocational training of these helpless destitute. The present judicial procedure leaves much to be desired. It is reported that on an average about 100 cases are disposed in less than fifteen minutes. The beggar's are not individually identified or questioned reducing the court work to a mere formality. Therefore, it is felt that there is a need of a full time courts (where number of beggars is huge) or part time courts (where number of beggars is small) for dealing, exclusively, with the cases of beggars, in detail and prescribe an appropriate line of treatment. As seen in number of cases the certified institutions are in worst conditions and not habitual for living, the new Act should make strict rules and procedures for maintenance of these institutions. In addition, the rehabilitation process provided in the acts is not up to the mark, as beggars who are being provided with vocational training are not much benefited. Further, the word "detention" be omitted and instead "admission or intake". Thus, the new act should be formulated, keeping all these facts in mind.

- Based on the empirical study it was found that the laws relating to beggary are not properly enforced, hence the provisions should be strictly implemented by the implementing agency. Therefore, it is suggested that for the better implementation of the Jammu and Kashmir Prevention of Beggary Act, 1960, a coordination mechanism for police and other enforcement agencies be promoted.
- The role of the judiciary to alleviate the plight of beggars and assist them to lead a dignified life should be a purposeful thrust. Thus, the courts in India have to play a vital role in eradicating this menace as well as to provide some sort of remedy to these destitute beggars. Further, the courts have to render justice within a reasonable time by protecting the weak from inhuman exploiters and at the same time delivering society from the bane of begging.
- There are various social welfare programs initiated at the central and state government levels. India has pumped in a lot of public money on NHM, MGNREGS, Bharat Nirman and Public Distribution System but poverty, unemployment and livelihood security have remained a major concern. Central and State government initiatives such as Mahatma Gandhi National Rural Employment Guarantee Act (MGNREGA) and it needs to be implemented effectively along with other schemes. The proper implementation of these schemes will result in poverty alleviation and enable the people to earn their livelihood. As a result of this people will not resort to the

menial ways of earning their livelihood like beggary is one.

- There should be formulation of a new national policy on beggars and a model legislation on beggary at the central level, which can be suitably adopted by States/UTs. There seems to be an urgent need to have an Integrated Programme for Rehabilitation of Beggars, which may include programmes like Night Shelter-cum-Work Production Centre; Multiple Skill Training; Mobile Health Care; Counseling; Awareness Generation; and Sensitization.
- Effective planning should be made by the government to solve unemployment and poverty. The government should create more and more employment opportunities in rural areas to arrest migration from rural to urban areas. In order to curb this problem, the government of India should introduce various schemes for the upliftment of beggars. Imparting education and creating employment for these marginalized sections for a viable solution to the problem.
- The state should provide facilities for free treatment of chronic diseases like leprosy and psychological ailments and open special clinics to take care of those who are unable to pay for treatment of these diseases for preventing forced begging.
- There is an urgent need to identify forced beggary rackets to punish their leaders instead of punishing beggars. Inquiry is to be conducted to identify and prosecute the criminals and members of the Beggar Mafia network. Public should check underground beggar organizations and they should be given capital punishment.
- All the orphans and handicapped should be taken care of by opening more and more rehabilitation centers, where general and technical education should be given to orphans. Institutional care or outdoor relief should be

given to the handicapped to enable them to get a better livelihood and live with dignity.

- The state needs to develop a multi- pronged approach for dealing with the problems of beggars who form multiple categories and keep on merging with economically & weaker sections. There cannot be one single solution for dealing with them, the approach should be "group oriented". Different groups are to be dealt with separately, within the parameters of different laws applicable to them.
- All the States where they have their own anti-beggary laws have constructed beggar homes (Certified Institutions) for the rehabilitation of beggars. However, according to the data available, most of the beggar homes remain unoccupied to the extent of 50 percent due to unhygienic conditions. Therefore, it is suggested that the concerned State Government should construct beggar home, sick home and children home, which fulfils all the necessary conditions suitable for them to lead a dignified life. The beggar homes that exist must be rendered habitable and hygienic.

REFERENCES

Abebe, T. "Earning a living on the margins: Begging, street work and the socio-spatial experiences of children in addis ababa," Geografiska Annaler, Series B: Human Geography, vol. 90, no. 3, pp. 271–284, 2008.

Adedibu, A. A., & Jelili, M. O. (2011). Package for controlling street begging and rehabilitating beggars and the physically challenged in Nigeria: Paper for policy consideration. Global Journal of Human Social Science, 11(1).

Ballet, J., A. Bhukuth, F. Rakotonirinjanahary and M. Rakotonirinjanahary, "Family rationales behind child begging in antananarivo," Population, vol. 65, no. 4, pp. 695-712, 2010.

Cama, K. H. (1945). Types of beggars. In D. J. Kumarappa (ed.),

Our beggar problem how to tackle it (pp. 1-11). Bombay: Fadma Publications Ltd .

Chaudhuri, S., 1987. Beggars of Kalighat, Calcutta. Calcutta: Anthropological Survey of India, (MHRD).

Cherneva, "Human trafficking for begging," Buffalo Human Rights Law Review, vol. 17, no. 25, pp. 25-73, 2011.

Cook, S. (2016, January 24). India Beggars and Begging Scams: What You Should Know.

Das, D. K. L., 1983. Evaluation of beggar problem in Tirupati. Social Defence, 19.

Demewozu, W. "Begging as a means of livelihood: Conferring with the poor at the orthodox religious ceremonial days in Addis Ababa, African study monographs," Supplementary issue, vol. 29, pp. 185-191, 2005.

Duneier, M., 1999. Sidewalk, Farrar Straus and Giroux, New York.

DWCWAP, 1980. Profile of Beggars in Hyderabad City: A Socio-Economic Study. Andhra Pradesh: Indian Council of Social Welfare.

Goel, A., 2010. Indian anti-beggary laws and their constitutionality through the prism of fundamental rights with special reference to Ram Lakhan V. State. Asia Pacific Journal on Human Rights and the Law, 11(1), 23-38.

Gore, M.S., Mathur, J.S., Laljani, M.R. & Takulia, H.S., 1959. The Beggar Problem in Metropolitan Delhi. Delhi: School of Social Work.

Goyal, O.P., 2005. Anti-Social Pattern of Begging and Beggars. Gyan Publishing House.

Kassah, K. "Begging as work: A study of people with mobility difficulties in Accra, Ghana," Disability & Society, vol. 23, no. 2, pp. 163–170, 2008.

Khan, J. (2013). Regional Analysis of Various Places of Begging. International Journal of Development Research, 3(10).

Khan, J. H., Menka, & Shamshad. (2013). "Beggars in rural areas: A socio-economic analysis". IOSR Journal of Humanities and Social Sciences, 122-129.

Khan, J. H., Menka, & Shamshad. (2013). Problems of Beggars: A Case Study. International Journal of Management and Social Science Research Review (IJMSRR) ISSN: 2319-4421, Volume 2, No. 12, December 2013, 2(12), 67-74.

Kumarappa, J.M. (Ed)., 1945. Our Beggar Problem: How To Tackle It?. Bombay: Padma Publications Ltd.

Moorthy, M.V., 1959. Beggar Problem in Greater Bombay: A Research Study. Bombay: Indian Conference of Social Work.

Mukharjee, R., 1945. Causes of beggary. In J. M. Kumarappa (Ed.), Our Beggar Problem: How To Tackle It. Bombay: Padma Publications Ltd, 19-26.

Mukherjee, D., 2008. Laws for beggars, justice for whom: A critical review of the Bombay prevention of begging act 1959. International Journal of Human Rights, 12(2), 279-288.

Namwata, M. L. M. R. Mgabo and P. Dimoso, "Categories of street beggars and factors influencing street begging in Central Tanzania," African Study Monographs, vol. 33, no. 2, pp. 133–143, 2012.

Prasad, L., 1960. Beggar problem in an Indian provincial town. The Indian Journal of Social Work, 21(2), 147-153.

Rafiuddin, D. (2012). Begging a Rs.200 crore industry in India .

Rafiuddin, M., 2008. Beggars in Hyderabad: A Study on Understanding the Economics of Beggary in Hyderabad; an Insight into Rehabilitation Possibilities. Andhra Pradesh: Hyderabad Council of Human Welfare.

Ramana, K.V. & Rao, P.K., 1973. No option but beggary. Social Welfare, 19 (10), 13-14.

Rao, T.S., & Bogaert, M.V.D., 1970. The beggar problem in Ranchi. The Indian Journal of Social Work, 31(3), 285-302.

Ratan, K., 1961.Beggar problem in Kanpur. The Indian Journal of Social Work, 21(4), 397-401.

Reddy, C. (2013). Begging and its Mosaic Dimensions: Some Preliminary Observations In Kadapa District Of Andhra Pradesh. Afro-Asian Journal of Social Sciences, 4(1).

Save the Children (2011) Regional report on child begging: Prevalence, prevention and suppression of child begging, South East Asia: Safe the Children.

Shah, N. (2011). Begging In India: Generously Putting Stop to It.

Shah, Nirav (2011, November 8). Beggary in India: Generously Putting Stop To It.

Siddique, M. (2008, Oct 10). Begging: A Rs 1.8 billion industry. Retrieved from http://www.rediff.com: http://www.rediff.com/money/2008/oct/10beg.htm

Thakker, Y. Gandhi, Z., Sheth, H., Vankar, G.K. & Shroff, S., 2007. Psychiatry morbidity among inmates of the beggar home. International Journal of Psychosocial Rehabilitation, 11(2), 31-36.

9

Globalised Economy and Women Development

INTRODUCTION

Gender equality is critical to the development process. The process of globalization may have resulted in new avenues of growth, but due to unequal distribution of its benefits women have been adversely affected in many cases. It calls for creating opportunities for women to be part of this development process. Merely enacting legislation will not solve the problems, but what is required is its proper implementation.

Globalization is a double framed process so far as women are concerned. On the one hand, majority of women in India and in other developing countries find themselves striped off the benefits of social security, government subsidies and then safety nets. On the other hand, there are possibilities of better education facilities and opportunities at the transnational sense, which are very attractive to the privileged few.

Capitalism's development across the globe has depended on a massive flood of millions of women into the workforce who had traditionally been reliant on husbands and male relatives. Globalization has contradictory effects on women. It has also brought great freedom to women, especially those living in traditionally conservative countries like Indonesia, Ireland and Thailand, where for the first time women are able to be economically independent of men and to have at least some choice in their personal lives. Ultimately, by bringing women into the workforce, globalization has given women a power that they had not enjoyed in the past, which generated the poverty, exploitation and oppression. Globalization may be denoted as a complex economic, political, cultural, and geographic process in which the mobility of capital, organizations, ideas, discourses, and peoples has taken a global or transnational form.

The IMF creates "one sided structural adjustment(s) involving the obliteration of real economic activity as well as attempts to create new forms of production bit without a corresponding destruction of financial capital and without a reconstruction of international financial flows" (Elson 1992).

Cultural influences in developing nations also influence employment stratification. Bringing a high demand of employment opportunities for women in developing nations creates an expeditious change within the social structure of these societies. Although the demand for female employment brings about an array of opportunities and sense of independence, the glass ceiling continues to exist with the "feminization of poverty" (Moghadam, 2005).

Corporations desire female labor for assembly production because women will "work in labor-intensive industries at wages lower than men would accept and in conditions that unions would not permit" (Moghadam.Valentine M, 1999).

When comparing occupations, "nearly two-thirds of women in manufacturing are categorized as laborers, operators and production workers while only a few can be found in the administrative and managerial positions predominantly held by men" (Tzannatos, Zafiris. 1999).

Economic globalization is a process tending towards neoliberal economic policy reforms (such as deregulation and privatization) and increases in capital, goods, services and workforce movement (Richards & Gelleny, 2007).

Economic theory on "globalization's impacts on growth and wellbeing" does seldom make distinctions between genders. It is frequently assumed that women will pay the cost of market liberalization by an unquestionable loss of jobs, or of high-income jobs. However, trade theory suggests that a growing international trade should benefit women, especially in developing countries (Bussmann, M; 2009).

Globalization will turn some into winners and others into losers. Examining whether economic globalization helps to improve some aspects of women's wellbeing or if it rather hurts them, is important for various reasons (Gray, Kittilson & Sandholtz, 2006).

Globalization will turn some people into winners and others into losers. The possibilities and benefits resulting from it are not an unalloyed good. "Women are neither mere and simple victims, nor free and unchained actors" (Mills, 1999). Nobel Prize winner Prof. Dr. Amartya Sen (Sen, 1999) considers an essential aspect in order to encourage a fair development and reduce the inequalities fostered by globalization is to concentrate on the active role of women's agency rather than only on women's well-being, as a way to promote social change. Women are thus seen as "dynamic promoters of social transformations that can alter the lives of both women and men".

The analytic frameworks of globalization do not address globalization by itself; it is rather taken for granted. This leads to the production and reproduction of a given orthodoxy, based on dichotomous thinking (local/cultural/traditional as female vs. global/economic/modern as male), which ignores the active role of women in the globalization process (Davids & Van Driel, 2009).

The objectives of this chapter are to analyze the basic concepts of globalization and globalised economy. Secondly, it throws light on the positive and negative impacts of globalization on gender equality. Thirdly, it tries to present some need based issues and basic facts of rural tribal women in Odisha with respect to globalised economy. Finally, in the concluding remarks it tries to give some suggestive recommendations for the economic development of the women.

The methodologies adopted in this chapter were in the line of collection of data and analyzing them to reach its desired objectives. Here the data were collected from the secondary sources and then by reviewing some literatures and some specific researches the outcomes have been placed in the paper. In addition to this, several focus group discussions were conducted among the development practitioners and researchers on the topic to enrich.

GLOBALIZATION: A NECESSARY CONDITION FOR ECONOMIC DEVELOPMENT

Globalization is a process, which involves economic integration, transfer of policies across borders that transmits knowledge; stabilize culture and establishment of a global market free from socio-political control. It is a process of transformation of regional or local phenomena into global ones. It is multi-dimensional and it directly or indirectly makes substantial impact on human life. Globalization can simply be defined as homogenization or integration of people, countries, their economies and cultures. It has led to the end of geography and death of distance. Several times, we are debating about the effect of globalization on Indian poverty level. According to an United Nations Development Fund for Women's report

(1997), over the past two decades the process of globalization has contributed to widening inequality within and among countries, coupled with economic and social collapse in parts of Sub-Saharan Africa and countries in transition like in eastern Europe. Concerning economic inequalities, women are seen to be exploited by transnational corporations with the consent of their governments. Trade liberalization policies have led to the decline of small-scale and subsistence farming in developing and less developed countries because western countries, sell heavily subsidized agricultural products to the developing or less developed countries. As a result, many female farmers who have been pushed of their land have sought employment in export processing zones, at lower wages than their male counterparts.

GLOBALIZATION AND GENDER PARITY

In the industrialized countries, the process of globalization bears a different impact on women than on men. Nevertheless, they are not affected as a group, but in different ways according to their class and ethnicity. Globalization affects different groups of women in different places in different ways. In one hand, it may create new opportunities for women to be forerunners in economic and social progress. With the introduction of global communication networks and cross-cultural exchange there seems to be a change in the status of women albeit not to a very large extent. However, globalization has indeed promoted ideas and norms of equality for women that have brought about awareness and acted as a catalyst in their struggle for equitable rights and opportunities. On the other hand it may exacerbate gender inequality in a patriarchal society, especially in the developing world. In the economic realm it may lead to further marginalization of women in the informal labour sector or impoverishment through loss of traditional sources of income.

India has some of the highest levels of sex discrimination at birth. According to 2017 analysis of demographic data, India will continue to have the worst sex ratio in south Asia. The 918 girls for 1000 boys' ratio (2011) have insisted government to take action in the form of 'Beti Bachao, Beti Padhao' programme to provide survival, safety and education to the girl child. All the factors strengthen the incentives for policy action towards gender equality around the world. However, in the absence of public policy, globalization alone cannot reduce gender disparity. The new forces associated with globalization understood as the combination of economic integration, technological diffusion and greater access to information have operated through markets, formal institutions and informal institutions to lift some of the constraints to greater gender equality. Trade openness and through new information and communication technologies more jobs have created and stronger connections to markets for many women have made and increased their access to economic opportunities.

Impact of Globalization on Women in India

By 1970, it became apparent that none of the promises made to women by the defenders of the development discussion were fulfilled in the Indian context and all over the world. Because of the dissatisfaction a new way of looking at women in the context of development began to take shape, this was called the 'Women in Development' approach.

Globalization and its Positive Impact on Women

Globalization provides opportunities for not only working men, but also women, who are becoming a larger part of the workforce. With new jobs for women, their self-confidence raise that must brings about independence. Globalization has the power to uproot the traditional views towards women so they can take an equal position in society. The impacts are as follows:

(i) **On income and employment**: Globalization has increased the exports of different countries and wages in export sectors are much higher than other sectors and in many cases women get higher wages than men get in formal industrial sectors. With globalization, women's employment opportunities have increase, and now they are also contributing in family expenses which support the creation of new resources and raise the level of income of family, though they are doing lot of family work without any wages.

(ii) **On Agriculture**: If the agricultural work is done with traditional methods, this trend has very serious gender implications. In small farms where crops are grown in traditional way, the demand for women's work is very high, but they are getting very low wages. The increase of profitability of cash crops in the international markets increases the independence of women. Because of globalization, there are structural changes in agricultural production. By working in family farms, women paid nothing or very squat wages but women get higher wages while working in companies especially in export industries. Women's are shouldering more than the double burden i.e working in the field as well as attending to household chores. The technology used in agriculture is making women to cope with the technology. Women in the urban settings have become more independent and self-sufficient.

(iii) **On Service Sector**: While talking about impact of globalization on women, we cannot ignore its impact of service sector. At present time, service sector is the most important sector. Some service sectors like communication and information technology are achieving the same progress achieved by industrial sector. Globalization has the power to uproot the traditional views towards women so they can take an equal stance in society. As India is an agriculturist country, women get many opportunities to increase their income level in agriculture sector. Women's ratio in agriculture work is more than as compared to men. In agriculture sector, women not only are getting benefits from industrial sector and service sector too. After the globalization has emerged, it has increased the living standard of people and especially for women.

Negative Impact on Women

Globalization has had negative connotations for Indian women. Their plights are similar to those of women in other developing regions such as Africa and Asia. World Development Indicators estimate that women work two-thirds of the world's working hours, produce half of the world's food, but earn only ten per cent of the world's income, and own less than one per cent of the world's property.

In the rural India, women have been independent and strong-headed. They have been the primary breadwinners in many cases. The society does want to accept the truth where women can be self-sufficient and need not rely on men for their survival. It is not asserting that women are free and empowered but certainly offering a fresh perspective that conveys to the western reader that women in the rural dwellings are more capable of taking care of themselves than in urban cities.

Globalization has had adverse effects on women especially in the developing countries. As consumers, women are increasingly facing a consumer culture which reduces them to commodities and as producers; women are exposed to work exploitation and occupational hazards. Prof. Amartya Sen, has rightly mentioned that disadvantages of women are not; of course, unique to India, and there is much evidence of extensive gender based inequality even in the elementary matters of health care and nutrition in many regions across the world. Nevertheless, detailed comparisons of mortality, morbidity rates, hospital care, nutritional attention etc. have been made in India, and they clearly confirm a decisive future for women being systematically deprived vis-à-vis men in India especially in rural area.

IMPACT OF GLOBALIZATION ON ODISHA

In case of Odisha, it is observed that instead of any positive impact numerous socio-cultural-economical problems entangled the rural and tribal women in the era of Globalization. Due to POSCO project in Jagatsingpur district. Large numbers of people under compulsion of forcibly displaced for the mega project. They have been deprived of their traditional source of perennial income. Since last 12 years except 2700 acres of land acquisition nothing has been done so far for the steel project is concerned. Similarly in the case of Vedanta Alumina project in Lanjigarh of Kalahandi district, after the direction of Hon'ble Supreme Court special Grama Sabha were held and accordingly people rejected the proposal of Odisha government to lease Niyamgiri Bauxite hill to Vedanta Companies. The Dangaria Kandha shows an example how they united to fight against the unholy nexus between companies and Odisha goernment who made all sort of illegal attempts to displace the Dangeria tribal's and want to deprive them from their home and earth. Apart from it lack of employment opportunities in Odisha the rural people of Ganjam, Kalahandi, Bolangir, Nuapara, Kandhamal, Koraput, Sonepur, Baragarh are compel to migrate to neighbor states like Andhra Pradesh, West Bengal, Gujrat, Karnatak, Kerala and Tamilnadu to work there as migrant labour and forced labour. A report of the Govt. of Odisha indicates how in recent years women and children along with labour force of rural Odisha is facing numerous challenges for their food and fodder. The Tata Project in Ganjam, Kalinga Nagar steel project in Jajpur district, Vedanta companies, private university in Puri etc. makes the rural people nowhere. Far from any visible positive impact, Odia rural economy suffers lot and is going to be paralyzed if the same trend continues for another decade or so.

WOMEN WORKERS AND GLOBALISED ECONOMY

The global development of capitalism over the last 20 years has depended almost everywhere on women pouring into the formal workforce. From Dublin to Dhaka, Bangkok to Bradford, women workers have provided the cheap labour from which super-profits have been extracted.' The following table shows the extent to which women workers have provided the new labour force in both the Asian and Celtic 'Tiger' economies. The number of women in the workforces has almost doubled in these countries over the last two decades.

Increase in Number of Female Workers 1980-1999 (in 1000's)

Countries	1980	1985	1990	1995	1997	1999
Indonesia	16,934.6	22,506.5	29,422.7	31,729.0	33,079.0	n/a
Ireland	346.4	332.0	371.5	482.9	539.7	643.9
Thailand	10,657.0	10,749.1	14,386,2	14,795.2	15,041.3	14,365.9
Korea	5,222.0	5,833.0	7,376.0	8,256.0	8,686.0	8,303.0
Philippines	6,070,0	7,569.0	8,185.0	9,505.0	19,451.0	11,709.0

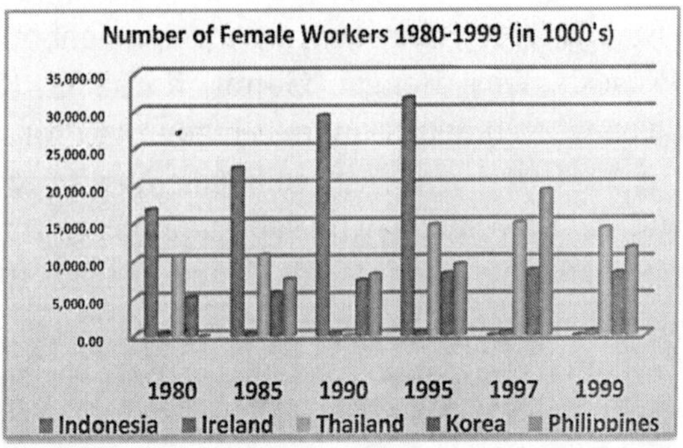

Globalization and Status of Rural/Tribal Women at National Scenario

- Modern rapid industrialization due to globalization after 1990's results in the decline of household industries. Since they constitute biggest traditional source of women's employment outside agriculture and rural women are the greatest victims of this process of economic transformation.
- The technological changes and unskilled nature of women labour exclude them from industrial sector. Absence of any rule or authority to enforce women's rights leads to their exploitation.
- It is found that women are low earning groups having low skill and technology, besides the level of education and employment opportunities for rural women is considerably decreased which affects their role and status in society.
- The committee on status of women in India projected that nearly 94 percent of women are engaged in unorganized sector of the economy, 81.4 percent being in agricultural occupations, almost half of the rural women works as agricultural labourers and they are the source of cheap labour. In this era of globalization, their work goes undervalued in an economy that puts premium on marketable work.
- Women dominate the traditional subsistence sector; the development process ignores their contribution. Modernization and globalization deprives them their status as producers and providers of families. Generally, it is believed that all the process of modernization and technological advancement is equally good for both men and women but in rural areas, even the introduction of simplest machine that adds to the skill of a man deprives the women in the absence of proper training opportunities.
- It is argued that even as globalization provides benefits and opportunities for many thus threatening livelihoods

and survival. It can be stated that globalization in future likely to increase 'Skill selectivity' as economic sectors become more receptive to information technologies and bio-technologies thus adversely affect those without such skills particularly the rural women.

- Today rural women have lost their original world under the impact of industrialization. Massive commercialization of minor forest product and large-scale deforestation diminished their economic role and lead to severe stress on her economic backbone.
- The agricultural land in rural areas is taken away from the people with low compensation to established industries without providing any permanent source of income, which affects the women more than the men.
- Globalization leads to prostitution, illegal trafficking of young girls, women from rural and poor family by pretty man for flesh trade which is now recognized in certain countries like Indonesia as sex tourism. It is a serious crime against women in the name of earning foreign currency and globalizing contagious diseases.
- The traditional role of women in agriculture livestock and animal husbandry, khadi and village industries including handicrafts, handlooms fisheries, etc, is being undermined because mechanization and automation is becoming prevalent in the market based economy which adversely affect the rural women.
- Privatization and reduction of public services will reduce regular employment opportunities for women as it increased the low paid, part-time, exploitative jobs and worse working conditions.
- Privatization of education and training will increase the cost of getting education. When family budget are readjusted, the female children will be in problems because most of the resources will be spent to educate male children.

- Because of globalization, health, migration, employment and environmental problems are rising. Specifically it affects rural, tribal and dailt women largely as they are the soft target of the government.
- Globalization for Indian women could have been interpreted as amelioration of women's status, decline in her fertility, obligations, reduction in her mortality and contraception burdens her empowerment for that could be overcome her predicaments and her active participation in all democratic institutions of society to ensure equity and justice.

CONCLUSION

It can be analyzed that globalization is neither good nor bad in itself. However, it may be positive for someone and negative for others, on the basis of how they are able to manage the process. The roles of women in India have been changing and they are now emerging from the past traditions into a new age of freedom and rights due to globalization. Women have made great march in the corporate world, but still the patriarchal nature of Indian society stops from having careers that infringe too much on family life. Women are now supporting their families with dual incomes thereby increasing the voice not only at home but also at parliament for 50 percent reservation. It has been seen that 'even in this century, the women are being exploited, but they may not raise their voices; not even against the sexual harassment they may face in the work place. Globalization provided with increasing opportunities to work for women in solidarity at regional, national and international levels to demand their rights. Their objective is to help promote mechanisms that strengthen the positive aspects and consequences of globalization, especially with respect to women's rights and gender equality'.

Globalization has changed the intra-household

responsibilities for males and females, where females are given more responsibility over the survival of the family. The limited advanced of women in the formal sector shows a great disregard for their social and economic responsibilities within developing nations. Female labor is not rewarded in relation to the impact they have on society. Therefore, women's work continues to be stigmatized as inferior, in comparison to males work, regardless of their increased responsibilities in society.

Globalization offers women unmatched opportunities, but equally new and unique challenges. Gender inequality spirals from many sources, and it is often difficult to determine which forms of inequality are being eliminated by the effects of globalization, and which are intensified. Work toward eliminating gender inequality in the framework provided by the Beijing Platform for action has created awareness, monitoring, and alleviation of the externalities that the new global system creates for women. Progress toward eliminating gender inequality in the future depends on finding and embracing the occasions, mostly in the political and legal realm, where the global approach strengthens women's security and welfare, and fighting the issues, mostly in the economic realm, where women are made worse off by the new global system.

In several cases, women are bread winner for family but society does not want to accept this truth. The culture of India is like that most of people thought that if a woman chooses to be a working women, it will adversely affect their family and children. In many cases, it is not true so. A women career would not be at the cost of disregard the family and children. At last, the truth is that globalization is unleashing competition between women and men.

There are some abiding features of the economic reform process like reduced role of the state in forestry and greater and easier access to international markets for poor women's products. Enabling the advancement of female opportunities and guaranteeing female workers more rights will increase the quality of life and create a more sustainable living standard for women and their families in the developing world. Without these changes, women will continue to suffer in their subordinate positions within the economic market.

Everyone in the developing world remains more susceptible to poor health because of lack of services or lack of access to services, and a lack of education and information about health issues. To wipe out these problems, the World Bank emphasizes public education programs that promote healthy lifestyles, eliminate gender discrimination in education and access to services, and prioritize the help for young girls. Therefore, the investments that improve women's health and nutrition are justified on both economic and humanitarian grounds, because they serve to alleviate poverty and develop human resources.

Women's empowerment does not just include aspects such as education, access to land or capital ownership, opportunities in the labor market or the nature of their employment contracts, but also family and social attitude towards the economic activities performed by women, and the social or economic circumstances supporting those attitudes or preventing them from changing. These issues have a direct bearing on women's well-being but their reach goes beyond that and it should be taken care of.

According to a United Nations Development Fund for Women's report, over the past two decades the process of globalization has contributed to widening inequality within and among countries, coupled with economic and social collapse in parts of sub-Saharan Africa and countries in transition like in Eastern Europe and the former Soviet Union and financial crises in Asia and Latin America. The process of globalization must be reshaped so that it is more people-centered instead of profit-centered and more accountable to women.

In the last decade, there has been an important process to try to alleviate almost all the negative aspects. Form a legal perspective, the enactment of regulation and the establishment of several international organizations have meant a substantial effort and proposed different alternatives.

The first major concern is that globalization leads to a more unequal distribution of income among countries and within countries. The second fear is that globalization leads to loss of national sovereignty and those countries are finding it increasingly difficult to follow independent domestic policies. These issues have to be addressed theoretically and empirically.

The globalization process is clearly a lopsided prescription and emerging economies/developing countries have to negotiate and put then food down for reciprocal gains. Otherwise, globalization will, in its present form, raise GDP statistics, but not the welfare of the masses. Absolute poverty may and has reduced to some extent but relative poverty will increase due to increasing disparities of income distribution and job opportunities. Therefore, the plans and policies must be devised accordingly to achieve the targeted objectives.

The forces of globalization are creating barriers for Tribal people to come together to identity and acknowledge commonality. Tribal people who do not have enough education, health and nutrition to compete in the competitive scenario are bound to fall outside the cutthroat competition in the market therefore, equal distribution of assets, income, credit, power, knowledge and skills are important to market to work more efficiently. Special policy and programmes are required to address and redress these differences especially in the context of globalization.

The negative outcomes of globalization should not be

superimposed on a poorly educated and poorly trained tribal people with poor systems of governance and infrastructure; it would not lead to growth nor reduce poverty.

A new development model needs to be created wherein responsibilities of social development will equally shoulder by both government as well as private players individually and collectively. Hence, the government should frame special policy and programmes that are required to address these differences especially on the context of globalization.

When we plan for tribal development, we have to take a special note of their situations and capabilities and provide them facilities to develop on the line they want to take. Globalization may no longer be an option, but a fact. However, 'it must be implemented with a human face. It is necessary to understand that outsiders cannot develop tribal's; they can become only facilitators if they want to do so'.

Till date, the rate of achievement of universal primary education in the context of ST children is very dismal. Unless clarity and a conscious recognition of the extent of problems and the complexities involved with delivery of primary education by the state and its institutions are brought out for a national debate and planning, utilizing the constitutional rights provided by the Act for achieving free and compulsory education for ST children would remain unfulfilled.

In Odisha the quality of services provided to the population by both public and private sectors is questionable. The current structure of the health care delivery system does not provide enough incentives for improvement in efficiency. Mechanisms used in other states to produce greater efficiency compare to Odisha, accountability and more responsible governance in hospitals are not yet deployed in Odisha. Current policies and standards setting process for health is inadequate or non responsive to ensure health services of acceptable quality and prevent negligence and hence it must be pro people, need based and area specific.

Bibliography

Bagchi, A. Globalisation, Liberalisation and Vulnerability Indian and Third World, Economic and Political Weekly, 34 (48), 3219-30

Bradley, K., & Khor, D. (1993). Toward an integration of theory and research on the status of women. Gender & Society, 7(3), 347–378.doi:10.1177/089124393007003003

Bunch, Charlotte and Roxanna Carrillo. 1990. "Feminist Perspectives on Women in Development." Pp. 70-82 in Persistent Inequalities: Women & World Development, Irene Tinker, editor. New York: Oxford University Press.

Bussmann, M. (2009). The effect of trade openness on women's welfare and work life. World Development, 37(6), 1027–1038. doi:10.1016/j.worlddev.2008.10.007

Chibberm B. (2002); Globalisation and its Impact on Women: A Critical Analysis, Mainstream, May 9, XLVII (21).

Dash, S. K., Political Empowerment of Tribal Women, Sonali Publication, New Delhi 2012.

Davids, T & Van Driel, F. (2009). The unhappy marriage between gender and globalization.Third World Quarterly, 30(5), 905–920.doi:10.1080/01436590902959107.

Desai, Manisha. 2002. Transnational Solidarity: Women's Agency, Structural Adjustment and Globalization. Pp. 15-33, New York: Routledge.

Elson, Diane. 1992. From Survival Strategies to Transformation Strategies: Women's Needs and Structural Adjustments. Pp. 26-48 ; Westview Press.

Gray, M. M., Kittilson, M. C & Sandholtz, W.(2006). Women and globalization: A study of 180 countries,1975-2000. International Organization, 60, 293–333.

Mills, M. B. (1999). Thai women in the global labor force. New Brunswick, NJ: Rutgers University Press.

Moghadam, Valentine M. 1999. "Gender and Globalization: Female Labor and Women's Mobilization." Journal of World Systems Research, 2: 367-388.

Moghadam, VM (July 2005). The 'feminization of poverty' and women's human rights . SHS Papers in Women's Studies/ Gender Research: 39.

National Council for Women, Women & Globalization, Seminar, Cairo, May 2001.

Odisha Economic Survey 2008-09. Directorate of Economics and Statistics, Planning and Coordination Department, Odisha.

Odisha HDR 2004. Odisha Human Development Report, 2004. Planning and Coordination Department, Odisha.

Panda, M., Poverty in Odisha: A Disaggregated Analysis, paper for the NCCDS workshop on poverty monitoring, Bhubaneswar, February 2002.

Porpora, D V L and U Prommas, The Role of Women in the International Division of Labour: The Case of Thailand, in Development and Change, vol. 20 (1989).

Prieto-Carrón, M. (2008). Women workers, industrialization, global supply chains and corporate codes of conduct. [Springer.]. Journal of Business Ethics, 83, 5–17. doi:10.1007/s10551-007-9650-7

Rajput, Pam (ed.) (1994); Globalisation & Women, New Delhi, Ashish Publishing House.

Ramos, S., 'Institutionalised Violence Against Women and the Code of Ethics', speech at conference on 'Global Standards in Focus', 13-15 October 2000.

Richards, D. L., & Gelleny, R. (2007). Women's status and economic globalization. International Studies Quarterly, 51, 855–876. doi:10.1111/j.1468-2478.2007.00480.

Sacks, K, 'Engels Revisited: Women, the Organization of Production and Private Property' in R Reiter (ed), Towards an Anthropology of Women (New York, 1975).

Schultz, T. Paul. 1990. "Women's Changing Participation in the Labor Force: A World Perspective." Economic Development and Cultural Change, 38 (3): 457-487.

Sen, A. (1999). Development as freedom. Westminster, MD: Alfred A Knopf.

Sen, K, 'Indonesian Women at Work: Reframing the Subject', in K Sen and M Stivens (eds), Gender and Power in Affluent Asia (London, 1998), p40.

Tzannatos, Zafiris. 1999. "Women and Labor Market Changes in the Global Economy: Growth Helps, Inequalities Hurt, and Public Policy Matters" World Development, 3: 551-569.

United Nations Development Fund for Women. (2000). Progress of the world's women 2000:United Nations Development Fund for Women Biennial Report. New York, NY: United Nations.

Ward, Katharine. 1990. Women Workers and Global Restructuring, New York: Cornell University Press. (Introductory chapter).

Wolf, D L, 'Linking Women's Labor with the Global Economy', in K Ward (ed), Women Workers and Global Restructuring (New York, 1990).

Wright, S. (1995). Women and the global economic order: A feminist perspective. The American University Journal of International Law and Policy, 10 (2), 861–887.

Index